This book is one of a series of studies of Jewish community organization prepared by the Center for Jewish Community Studies of the Jerusalem Center for Public Affairs. English language studies in the series to date include:

The Balkan Jewish Communities: Yugoslavia, Bulgaria, Greece, and Turkey

    by Daniel J. Elazar, Harriet Pass Friedenreich, Baruch Hazzan, and Adina Weiss Liberles (1983)

Community and Polity: The Organizational Dynamics of American Jewry

    by Daniel J. Elazar (Jewish Publication Society, 1976)

The French Jewish Community by Ilan Greilsammer (forthcoming)

The Governance of Canadian Jewry edited by Harold M. Waller and Daniel J. Elazar (1983)

Jewish Communities in Frontier Societies: Argentina, Australia and South Africa

    by Daniel J. Elazar with Peter Y. Medding (Holmes and Meier, 1983)

The Jewish Communities of Scandinavia: Sweden, Denmark, Norway, and Finland

    by Daniel J. Elazar, Adina Weiss Liberles, and Simcha Werner (1983)

THE JEWISH COMMUNITIES OF SCANDINAVIA

SWEDEN, DENMARK, NORWAY AND FINLAND

Daniel J. Elazar
Adina Weiss Liberles
and Simcha Werner

UNIVERSITY
PRESS OF
AMERICA

Center for Jewish Community
Studies of the Jerusalem
Center for Public Affairs

LANHAM • NEW YORK • LONDON

University Press of America,™ Inc.

4720 Boston Way
Lanham, MD 20706

3 Henrietta Street
London WC2E 8LU England

Co-Published by arrangement with the
Center for Jewish Community Studies/
Jerusalem Center for Public Affairs

ISBN(Perfect): 0-8191-3472-4
ISBN (Cloth): 0-8191-3471-6

All University Press of America books are produced on acid-free
paper which exceeds the minimum standards set by the National
Historical Publications and Records Commission.

This volume is dedicated to the staff of the Jerusalem Center for Public Affairs whose devoted efforts have built the Center into a serious factor on the contemporary Jewish scene in a few short years.

CONTENTS

This volume is a product of the worldwide study of Jewish Community organization conducted since 1968 and under the auspices of the Center for Jewish Community Studies since its founding as the Jewish Community Studies Group in 1970. The Center for Jewish Community Studies is a research and educational institute devoted to the study of the organized Jewish community, past and present, and to the dissemination of its findings through teaching and publication, with a view toward enhancing the knowledge base used in making public policy decisions within Jewish life. The Center is built around a group of Fellows and Associates drawn from academic institutions in Israel and throughout the world, and maintains offices in Jerusalem, Philadelphia, and Montreal. Since 1976, it has operated within the framework of the Jerusalem Center for Public Affairs.

The Study of Jewish Community Organization, one of the Center's principal projects, is a worldwide study of the dynamics of governance of all the organized countrywide Jewish communities presently in existence as they have been reconstituted since World War II. The initial effort within its framework was the "mapping" of the structures and functions of the organized Jewish communities in the world, a task never before undertaken. The studies in this volume were prepared in the mid-1970s as part of that effort. Research for the studies in this volume was conducted in three of the four countries involved and in Jerusalem on several occasions between 1968 and 1979, hence they reflect the situation at the end of the postwar generation. As planned, they are in the nature of community maps which focus on communal structures and functions rather than full-fledged studies. The latter we have saved for the second stage of the research.

The authors would also like to extend their thanks to the staff of the Jerusalem Center for Public Affairs for their assistance in bringing this volume to print. Special thanks are due Hannah Klieger and Hollis Dorman of the Philadelphia office and Judy Cohen in Jerusalem, Sarah Lederhendler and Linda Shor for their typing of manuscripts through their various versions; and Amy L. Lederhendler for editorial direction in Jerusalem.

DJE, AWL, SW
Jerusalem
Kislev 5743 - December 1982

THE JEWRIES OF SCANDINAVIA

Daniel J. Elazar

On the European Fringe

For Jews as well as for others, Scandinavia has long been the European periphery, a frontier region in the sense that frontiers are borderlands—in this case the borderlands of a great continent—yet not quite a frontier in the sense of the cutting edge of civilization. While Scandinavia was long at the edge of Christian civilization in Europe, it has been Christianized for nearly a millenium. For Jews, on the other hand, the Scandinavian countries have consistently been at the outer edge or beyond and remain so to this day. In fact, Jewish settlement in the Scandinavian countries is entirely a modern phenomenon begun after the middle of the seventeenth century and insignificant even in the most relative terms until the late nineteenth.

Because of its peripheral location, it is only with the collapse of the modern era in the Gotterdamerung of World War II and in the events of the first generation of the post-modern era that Scandinavia has even risen to a position of notice on the Jewish map. A very modest number of Jews took refuge there with the rise of Nazism. The famous Danish rescue of its Jewish population has become almost legendary. The Scandinavian countries, particularly Denmark and Sweden, took in a few thousand refugees after World War II and a few thousand more fleeing from the Communist countries after the various troubles of the 1950's and 1960's. These actions, taken together have made the region somewhat more prominent in contemporary Jewish history than it ever was in the past. However, considering that the whole region contains less than 25,000 Jews out of a total population of somewhat in excess of 22 million, or far fewer Jews than the American state of Minnesota (34,000 out of 3.5 million), which is well-known as the heartland of Scandinavian settlement in the United States but possesses only one-seventh of the population of Scandinavia proper, speaks for itself.

Take the matter of settlement. Most European Jewish communities west of the Rhine were founded after 1605; however, those founded south of the Baltic region essentially represented the return of Jews to the countries and regions from which they had been expelled centuries before. This is true whether we consider Hamburg in Germany, London in England, or Bordeaux in France, to name but a few of the best known refounded Jewish communities. In the case of Scandinavia, the Jewish communities founded in those years were truly new ones and represented first time Jewish settlement, as much as the Jewish settlement in New Amsterdam (now New York) founded in 1654 (incidentally, before any Jewish community in Scandinavia). In sum, organized Jewish life did not reach Scandinavia until the beginning of the modern era and it is unlikely that more than an occasional stray Jewish individual did either.

Unlike the Western European and New World settlements, the Jewish communities of the north never attracted significant numbers of Jews even though they benefitted from the modern attitude toward Jews and Judaism as much as, if not more than, any of the other communities. Thus the Jewish communities of Scandinavia remained few, scattered and small outposts of Jewish life, off center stage even for emancipated Jews seeking their fortunes, not to speak of Jews desirous of preserving traditional Jewish lives. The history of Scandinavian Jewry can be summarized as one of the successive small waves of settlers coming in at times when some compelling reason, usually involving persecution and the search for a refuge, turned them northward, followed by periods of establishment and assimilation. As the studies of the individual countries indicate, the number of Scandinavian families recognizing their Jewish ancestry far exceeds the total number of Jews in their respective countries. Only the coming of successive waves of new settlers, small as they might have been, prevented the total assimilation of the existing Jewish communities.

Despite their out-of-the-way status, Scandinavian Jewries have followed patterns which are reminiscent of European Jewry as a whole and even of world Jewry to the extent that modernity has created certain common patterns for all Jewish communities. The initial impetus for Jewish settlement in Scandinavia came as a result of the spread northward of the Marranos searching for economic opportunity and peaceful places to rest. For the first century and a half of their existence, roughly from the middle of the seventeenth century until the Napoleonic wars, such Jewish communities as existed in Scandinavia were organized along the lines of other late medieval communities as autonomous kehillot whose authority and status were guaranteed by royal charter.

With the coming of emancipation at the beginning of the nineteenth century, the kehillot lost their autonomy. All were reorganized as more limited religious communities in return for which the Jews gradually gained full citizenship in the respective states of their residence. The first half of the nineteenth century was marked by a struggle for civil rights, while the last half was marked by a dual struggle against anti-Semitism and assimilation.

In Scandinavia as elsewhere in Europe, the Holocaust was the culmination of emancipation. The Nazi madness affected Scandinavian Jewry without destroying it. The overwhelming majority of the Jews of Scandinavia were either residents of neutral Sweden, beneficiaries of the Danish evacuation, or were protected by Finland which, as an ally of the German Reich, maintained control over its own indigenous population (the spectacle of Finnish Jewish officers serving side by side with the German army in the war against Russia was one of the more disconcerting phenomena of the war). Only the tiny Norwegian Jewish community felt the brunt of Nazi genocide. Indeed, because of the refugees who found their way north, the Scandinavian communities were actually enriched Jewishly as a result of World War II.

Subsequently, the post-war period brought with it the standard "bundle" of Jewish problems and opportunities. Jewish life again teeters between assimilation and survival; Jewish ties have become primarily associational, replacing traditional systems of belief and patterns of behavior; Israel has become a focal point stimulating Jewish survival yet draining off many of those most committed to Jewish life. Scandinavian Jewry is probably better organized than ever before in its history while at the same time its Jews are increasingly less Jewish in an organic sense.

Regional Collaboration

The Scandinavian countries, with the exception of Finland, share a common Nordic linguistic and cultural heritage. Finland, whose population is ethnically different, has been tied to Scandinavia because of its geographic proximity reinforced by a shared political history. While today all four Scandinavian countries (plus Iceland, the Scandinavian frontier) are politically independent states under international law, at various times they have been united in various combinations. The rise of modern nationalism led to their successful pursuit of national independence but the subsequent development of the need for international cooperation brought them together through a series of transnational links, principally the Nordic Union, to give them something short of confederation but more than a collection of ad hoc sharing arrangements.

This pattern is repeated in the Jewish world of Scandinavia, whereby the four small communities (Iceland has few Jewish families and no organized Jewish life) have created for themselves certain transcommunal institutions and ties.

With less than 28,000 Jews among them, there is every incentive for them to pool their resources and talents for common purposes. Consequently, a number of common institutions have developed embracing all of Scandinavian Jewry. While these institutions remain auxiliary to the local communities, they do play a necessary role. In the 1950's, a pan-Scandinavian Zionist Federation was active; its primary activity was the coordination of charter flights to Israel, the proceeds of which provided funds for scholarships to send Scandinavian Jewish youth to study in the Jewish state. When the charter flights were abolished, the federation became essentially inactive except for sponsoring an occasional seminar on a pan-Scandinavian basis.

WIZO (Women's International Zionist Organization) also tries to develop some of its activities on an all-Scandinavian basis to give Jewish women, particularly those in the smaller communities, a sense of belonging

to something larger than their local chapters. Since
1947, Inter-Nordic WIZO Conferences have regularly
been held on an alternating basis in Goteborg, Oslo,
Helsinki, and Stockholm, representing members in
Sweden, Denmark, Norway and Finland. WIZO tries to
activate such pan-Scandinavian activities in order to
provide a sense of belonging for its members, no
matter how small or unorganized their local Jewish
communities may be (if they exist at all). In many
communities WIZO constitutes the only real form of
Jewish affiliation available. It, too, seems to have
been more active in this regard in the 1950's. WIZO
makes some decisions on an all-Scandinavia basis.
Thus in 1963, its annual conference voted to admit
non-Jewish women to membership provided they had close
connections to Judaism (apparently meaning that theur
husbands were Jewish).

Bnei Akiva is the principal Jewish youth group
active in the Scandinavian countries. It is pan-
Scandinavian in its organization and its Executives
also sit in leading Jewish centers on a rotating
basis. It maintains a full-time Scandinavian shaliach
and rotates its main office between Stockholm and
Copenhagen. Its camps and seminars are usually
conducted on a Pan-Scandinavian basis and attract many
more young people than actually belong to the organization. These pan-Scandinavian programs, including
camps for the younger and older youth, camping in
Israel, and hachsharah, involved some 200 young people
annually in the mid-1970's.

The Jewish Agency also conducts many of its activities on a pan-Scandinavian basis. Its Youth and
Hechalutz Department has at various times sponsored a
one-year program in cooperation with the Paul Baerwald
School of Social Work in the Hebrew University to
train British and Scandinavian Jewish communal workers
(a program which was recently discontinued because of
lack of British candidates); provided an annual

leadership seminar in Scandinavia; and worked with other bodies, including the local Jewish communities of Scandinavia, in the development of a Jewish pedagogical and resource center in Malmo to translate educational materials, develop an audio-visual center, and create courses of study for Scandinavian Jews.

Aside from the Zionist activities, the World Jewish Congress maintains a regional office in Stockholm which is essentially designed to serve all of Scandinavia--in fact, it is a one-man enterprise and is limited accordingly. Thus B'nai Brith lodges in Sweden are united through the Scandinavian B'nai Brith Board and all members receive the Scandinavian B'nai Brith periodical <u>B'nai</u> <u>Brith</u> <u>Nyt</u>.

Youth Organizations

The SJUF is the all-Scandinavian youth organization. Its main goal is to prevent assimilation among Scandinavian youth, by providing a positive base of identification among the youth. Secondary aims are to support Israel and prevent anti-Semitism. Both students and non-students belong to the organization. All Jewish youth and student organizations in Scandinavia are affiliated with it, at least nominally. It holds an annual congress. Its office also rotates between Sweden and Denmark with the majority of the SJUF executive at any given time composed of members of the host community. It is formally sponsored by the World Jewish Congress, the local communities, and the World Union of Jewish Students, and tries to represent a united voice of youth in the adult community.

SJUF was founded in 1919 by Aron Grusd of Oslo and was active in the inter-war period. Its work was interrupted by the war, but after the war it resumed its efforts and, in the early 1950's, had 2,000 members representing almost ten percent of the total Jewish population of Scandinavia at the time. Its leadership has generally consisted of young adults who have later moved on to leadership of the Scandinavian Jewish communities.

SJUF was probably a much more active group twenty-five years ago than it is today. Now its main achievements have been the organization of three annual youth camps--two for teenagers and one for young adults (over eighteen years of age), at which time the annual SJUF Conference is held. In addition, periodic lectures, seminars, and conferences are held throughout Scandinavia. SJUF fosters identification with Israel, maintaining a branch office there which prepares educational programs for use in the various countries. Study courses in Hebrew and Jewish history have been developed through SJUF.

The Future of Scandinavian Jewry

Since they reside in one of the most affluent regions of the world, the Jews of Scandinavia are no better candidates for aliyah to Israel than those in the other affluent countries. The exceptions are that relative handful of young Jews who seek fuller Jewish lives and recognize that they cannot live as Jewishly as they wish in the small, assimilated communities of their home countries. They may try Israel and, if religiously Orthodox, are likely to settle. Those who come for what are generally called Zionist motivations are frequently discouraged and return. There may indeed be a lower rate of immigration of Scandinavian Jews than of Scandinavian non-Jews who, in the course

of a summer or year-long work experience in the kibbutz, meet and marry Israelis. While there is a
certain irony in the situation, it also serves to
somewhat redress the negative balance of intermarriage
in the Scandinavian countries themselves.

The historical record of the Scandinavian Jewish
communities time and again reaffirms the assimilationist tendencies of those communities. While
Scandinavia by no means has been free of anti-
Semitism, by and large it has still furnished a
climate that has encouraged individual Jews to abandon
their Jewishness and merge with the peoples among whom
they live. In this respect, the Scandinavian
countries have been quite open and have offered, for a
very small number of Jews, the possibilities of
assimilation that many advocates of Jewish
emancipation dreamed about. Only the periodic
infusion of new waves of immigrants has served to
revivify the Jewish communities of Scandinavia, either
by bringing in Jews of a more traditional bent or by
forcing the Jewish communities to activate themselves
to receive and care for the immigrants so as not to
call attention to the strangers being brought into the
midst of highly homogeneous societies.

It is this tendency to homogeneity which directs
the course of Jewish life in Scandinavia more than any
other external factor. The Scandinavian countries
have, in the course of their modernization, become
democratic and liberal, but they are not particularly
pluralistic for the simple reason that they do not have
highly heterogeneous populations. The Lapps are the
only large and distinctive ethnic minority in the
region, although each of the individual countries has
pockets of populations from one or more of the other
ones who often seek to preserve their language and
customs. Since those pockets generally represent
deeply rooted rural settlements, whose origins antedate
present state boundaries, they are in a different
category entirely. In the urban areas assimilation is

the rule. Under such conditions, a small minority such as the Jews is very vulnerable indeed.

The Jewish response has been characteristic of all modern Jewish communities. As Jews have shed their traditional habits, customs, and religion, except in their most public formalistic aspects, they have sought to substitute an associational framework, a manifestation of a culturally-based ethnicity. A culturally-based ethnicity implies some desire to maintain separate customs and minimize deep contacts with people outside one's own group. Scandinavian Jews hardly qualify in this sense. In fact, while those Jews who care about their Jewishness are concerned about intermarriage and seek to prevent it, they do not, for the most part, seek to associate exclusively with one another even outside of business hours. That would be most un-Scandinavian. Hence the Jewish communities do not exist as separated, ethnically closed groups.

In the nineteenth century, when formal religion was to have served as the associational bond to hold Jews together, the Jewish community was indeed a religious association, not particularly observant but still linked by formal religious ties. Since World War II, as the world and the Jews within it have moved more into the post-modern era, even this arrangement has broken down. Many young Jews are more than indifferent to religion; they reject it philosophically as do their non-Jewish Scandinavian (and for that matter European) peers.

What, then, remains for them as the basis for the maintenance of Jewish ties? Paradoxically, they, too, are increasingly bound to the Jewish people through what can only be termed political association. The nature of that political association is not yet fully clear or apparent, certainly not to those Jews themselves. Even the outside observer has not yet developed a full sense of it, but the combination of

xx

concern for and support of the State of Israel on one
hand, increasing reliance on the state as a Jewish
resource, and a pattern of association within the
Jewish community which makes those institutions which
are neither predominantly religious nor predominantly
welfare oriented most vibrant and attractive to
younger Jews, points strongly in the direction of this
conclusion. Thus, Scandinavian Jewry also reflects
one of the paradoxes of our times--the strange mixture
of full assimilation with Jewish identification
primarily on a political level that is coming to
characterize post-modern Jewry.

THE JEWISH COMMUNITY OF SWEDEN

Adina Weiss Liberles

Social And Historical Background

The Historical Development of Swedish Jewry

Jewish settlement in Sweden before the eighteenth century was very limited, due to generally negative government and church attitudes toward the Jews. A synagogue is said to have been built on the island of Marstrand in the Kallegat during the Middle Ages and Jewish paymasters joined the ranks of the army of King Charles XII, but by the seventeenth century baptism was the price of settlement in the country. In 1680 a small number of Jews in Stockholm (proving that Jews did live in Sweden unofficially for various periods of time) petitioned the government to rescind the conversion law, but it was not until 1718 that Jews were officially granted permission to settle in the country and still maintain their religious affiliation, and then only on condition that they restrict their settlement to the smaller cities and rural communities.

Aron Isaac, of Mecklenberg, arrived in Stockholm in 1774 and on May 2, 1775, received the permission of King Gustav III to settle there officially, thanks to the King's strong desire for his services as an engraver. Insisting upon the right to worship according to Jewish practice (in a minyan of ten adult Jewish males), Isaac was granted permission to form a small Jewish community. The first cemetery was consecrated in 1776 and three years later, Parliament, with full support of the King, granted settlement rights to be extended to Göteborg and Norrköping,

1

under certain conditions but with a considerable
degree of religious freedom.

Regulations passed by the Royal Office of Trade
and Commerce in 1782 broadened Jewish rights still
further. These laws were based on those in other
European nations, especially of Prussia, but were more
liberal than in most cases. Jews were permitted to
acquire real estate and engage in industry and trade
not affected by guild regulations. They were allowed
continued settlement in the three large communities
mentioned before and to build synagogues there. The
Jewish community was recognized as an autonomous
kehilla, regulating its own affairs with regard to
religious worship, welfare activities, inheritances,
guardianships and marriages within the community.
However, religious services were forbidden to contain
elements offensive to the general population, and
religious schools were forbidden, as were marriages as
a general rule between Jews and Christians;
furthermore, Jews, together with other non-Christians,
were ineligible for government posts and pensions and
could not vote. While the country's political leaders
defended and supported the Jews, the citizenry and the
church regarded them as rivals and intruders.
Anti-Semitic attitudes developed in Sweden, as
elsewhere throughout Europe, following the Napoleonic
Wars.[1]

The process leading to Jewish emancipation in
Sweden began with a royal decree issued by King
Charles XIV John and his Minister of Finance on June
30, 1838, repealing the restrictions of 1782 and
incorporating the Jews into the Swedish state. As a
consequence, the kehilla structure of an autonomous
colony of foreigners with well-defined rights was
abolished. In its place came Mosaic Communities, and
the Jews were called "adherents of the Mosaic faith."
Although restrictions on Jews were still retained in
the Constitution and the Swedish civil code, all
discriminatory administrative practices against them
were abolished. Once again the Swedish people's
reaction to the new liberalizing laws was vocal,
widespread, and critical, finally forcing the

2

government in September 1838 to repeal its permission for free Jewish settlement anywhere in the country, restricting it to Stockholm, Göteborg, Norrköping and Karlskrona.

During the next thirty years all remaining restrictions against the Jews were removed. First, in the 1840's, nearly all restrictions on Jewish trade and occupations were lifted, then, the bans on internal migration, intermarriage and municipal voting privileges. Finally, in 1870, Jews and Catholics were given the franchise and allowed to hold political office, although, until 1952, no one who was not a member of the Swedish Lutheran Church could hold a ministerial post.[2]

Although there were occurrences of anti-Semitism in the pre-Hitler period in Sweden, the general relationship between the Jewish and Christian populations remained cordial, with many Jews playing a role in the cultural life of the country. However, once Nazi policies began to be implemented in Germany, causing many Jews to emigrate, both the Swedish government and its citizens tried to block any large-scale Jewish immigration into the country.

As the war progressed, Swedish public opinion grew more favorable toward the refugees. The real turning point in Swedish immigration policy resulted from the Nazi invasion of Norway and the persecution of that country's Jews, between 700 and 900 of whom managed to escape to Sweden. Then, in October 1943, the Swedish government publicly offered asylum to fleeing Danes--Jewish and non-Jewish alike--and aided almost the entire Danish Jewish community, almost 8,000 persons, including non-Jewish Danish relatives, in settling within its borders for the duration of the war. It should be noted that the Jewish communities of both Sweden and Denmark took an active role in both organizing and financing resettlement. Furthermore, some of Stockholm Jewry's leadership were instrumental in arranging, through the auspices of the Swedish representative of the World Jewish Congress, a meeting between Norbert Mazur and

Heinrich Himmler in 1945, after which thousands more concentration camp victims were included in the rescue operations of Count Folke Bernadotte. Following the war, thousands more concentration camp inmates were brought to Sweden. It is estimated that slightly under half the Jewish population of Sweden today came as a result of World War II.[3]

In 1952, the Law of Freedom of Religion (the Dissenters' Act) abolished earlier Swedish regulations requiring its citizens to formally affiliate with some religious community. Until then, Jews could leave the community only by officially joining the State Church or another minority community. At first this law was cause for great concern among Swedish Jewry, who feared that many members would opt out of affiliation with the Jewish community once such participation became voluntary, causing deep financial problems for the community. However, these fears were apparently ungrounded, as only 350 Jews initially severed relationships. Moreover, once the community was transformed into a voluntary association, a large number of Jewish residents who were not Swedish citizens became eligible to affiliate with the community.[4] The Law of Freedom of Religion made it possible for Jews and other members of "special congregations" to occupy practically any post in Sweden, even the Premiership (the Minister of Education and Culture must still be a member of the Swedish Lutheran Church).

Waves of Immigrations

The majority of Jews immigrating to Sweden at the end of the eighteenth and first half of the nineteenth centuries came from Germany, most of whom engaged in banking, engraving, and trading (especially in the textile and tobacco industries). By the mid-nineteenth century the German Reform movement had made great progress in the Swedish Jewish community. The Göteborg community led the way to Reform under the leadership of its Chief Rabbi, Karl Heinemann

4

(1837-1868), and continued its growth under Stockholm's rabbi, Gottlieb Klein (1882-1944). David Schwarz claims that the attraction to Reform indicates a strong desire on the part of Swedish Jews to be better accepted within Swedish society by adapting their Jewish religious services to conform with Christian practice as closely as possible.[5] Most of the first Jewish families in Sweden disappeared through intermarriage and assimilation or a low birth-rate.

A new wave of Jewish immigration took place at the end of the nineteenth and the beginning of the twentieth centuries, this time from Eastern Europe, partly as a result of pogroms and the Russian Revolution. The East European Jews were more strongly opposed to assimilation, at least at the beginning, and revitalized the content of Jewish life in Sweden, supporting existing congregations and establishing new communities in the provinces (e.q. Malmö). Gradually, however, as their acculturation increased, their degree of Jewish identification declined. Census figures show that in 1880 the Jewish population in Sweden numbered 3,000; in 1910, 6,112; and that in 1930 there were 6,653 Jewish Swedish citizens and an additional 1,391 Jewish non-citizens residing in the country.

At the beginning of the twentieth century, the Jewish community of Stockholm attempted to persuade the Swedish Ministry of Transport to encourage East European immigrants to leave Sweden.[6] A similar phenomenon occurred in the 1930's, when the Stockholm Jewish community attempted to discourage Jewish immigration to Sweden, fearing an increase in the already existing Swedish anti-Semitism. In an address to the Swedish Parliament in January 1945, the Minister of Welfare stated, "The Swedish Government with regard to letting Jews come into the country was at least as generous as the Jewish community in Stockholm."[7]

However, we have seen how the Jewish community, the Swedish government, and finally the Swedish people

5

rallied behind the Jews once the Nazi policy of genocide became apparent. In 1938, the Swedish government tried to liberalize its immigration policy, but such an outcry was raised against liberalization by various labor and student groups that it was forced to once again tighten its restrictions; consequently, thousands of visas were denied, even when the Jewish community stood ready to personally guarantee the support of some of the immigrants. Following Kristallnacht (November 1938), 150 adults and 500 children without parents were admitted. By the outbreak of World War II, some 3,000 Jews had immigrated from Germany, Austria, and Czechoslovakia, in addition to about 1,000 others who passed through Sweden on route to other destinations and a few hundred halutzim who had been training in Sweden at the outbreak of the war.[8]

The Swedish people as a whole rallied behind the Norwegian Jewish refugees who fled to Sweden, the remnants of the Jewish community, most of which was destroyed in the extermination camps. The "Little Dunkirk" operation, bringing 93 percent of the Danish Jewish community, has been cited. In 1944, 250 stateless refugees came from Finland. Almost all Jews from the other Scandinavian countries returned home immediately following the war. Approximately 3,500 Jews were among the 20,000 refugees brought to Sweden through the efforts of Count Folke Bernadotte in Hungary. In June and July, 8,500 Jews, mostly from Bergen Belsen, were among the 10,000 refugees brought in by the Red Cross and UNRRA; almost all the latter group were East European Jewish women between 17 and 30 years of age. In the following two years another 3,300 refugees arrived, many of them hard core TB patients requiring immediate and intensive medical care. Altogether, some 20,000 refugees found asylum in Sweden during or after the war, the great proportion of whom were Jews. About 8,000 of the Jewish post-war refugees eventually emigrated to the United States, Israel, Canada, and South Africa, either with the help of international and Swedish Jewish relief organizations or by their own resources. The rest, between 2,500 and 3,000, became permanent

Swedish residents. Post-war refugee immigration continued until 1951.[9]

The absorption of the large numbers of refugees presented serious problems for the Swedish Jewish community, which levied additional income taxes on its members, half of which went for direct aid to the refugees. In addition, the Jewish women's groups opened kitchens, canteens, and conducted drives for clothing, utensils and dowries for the newcomers. Fifteen special schools were opened for refugee children. Financial aid provided by the Swedish government and the Swedish Jewish community was augmented by international Jewish funds, mostly from the American Joint Distribution Committee and later by the Conference on Jewish Material Claims Against Germany.

By the end of the 1950's, the majority of refugees who remained in Sweden were absorbed, at least from the economic and professional standpoints.[10] Social and cultural integration was much harder to achieve. New immigrants felt that the community had not made enough efforts to save Jews before the war began and in its early days; indeed, the Jewish Chronicle in 1947 carried several articles and letters accusing and defending the community.[11] Furthermore, new immigrants often felt that the Swedish Jews did not try to integrate the newcomers into the communal organizations and leadership positions. Whereas the older community was Swedish-speaking, Reform in religious practice, anti-Zionist and pro-assimilationist in philosophy, the new element was Yiddish-speaking, religiously more traditional and Zionist in leaning.

Most of the Jews who immigrated to Sweden after 1945 settled in smaller industrial towns or other small communities. Thus, a community like Boras, with about 350 Jews, reflects the Eastern European background.

The Hungarian Revolution in 1956 brought approximately 550 Jewish refugees to Sweden in the

7

years 1956-1957. The majority of these refugees were in their later middle age and many were physically or mentally ill. However, most of them eventually managed to integrate into the community comparatively well.[12]

Since the wave of Polish anti-Semitism in 1968, about 3,000 Polish Jews have immigrated to Sweden, settling mostly in industrial centers throughout the land, following the principles of the Swedish government on immigration and its efforts to prevent the growth of ethnic pluralism in Swedish society. However, in 1974, the government undertook to solve the problems of ethnic groups in Sweden by providing a budget to expand ethnic cultural activities, including those of the Jews.

Most of the Hungarian and Polish Jews admitted to Sweden were brought in on guarantees that they would not become public burdens. The Stockholm Jewish community has assumed financial responsibility for these immigrants.

The Demography of the Swedish Jewish Community

There are no definite figures for the number of Jews living in Sweden today. Estimates range between 15,000 and 17,000, an increase of between 2,000 and 3,000 Jews in the past ten years, reflecting the immigration from Poland. Between 7,000 and 8,000 Jews are estimated to reside in Stockholm, about 1,400 each in Mälmo and Göteborg; the rest are scattered throughout the country, in Boras (about 350-450), Nörrkoping (about 125), Köping (about twenty-five families), and smaller centers such as Lund, Örebro, Karlstad, Hälsingborg, Kristianstad, Kalmar, Eskilstuna, and Sundsvall.[13] According to 1961 population statistics, the Jewish population constituted 0.2 percent of the Swedish population. Over 5,000 Jews are considered veteran citizens (i.e., whose families arrived before 1933); over 2,000 are refugees from Germany and Austria who came between

8

1933-1939; about 5,500 are Eastern European survivors of concentration camps, about 500 are refugees from the Hungarian Revolution of 1968; and about 3,000 are refugees from Poland after 1968.[14]

Due to the stable character of social, political and economic life in Sweden and the absence of discrimination, Jewish emigration has been limited since 1951, except for a group originally from Rumania and a small percentage of those from Hungary and Poland. From the end of World War II to 1956 the community operated an emigration office. Today, a few Jewish families emigrate to the United States and there is a small stream of aliyah to Israel, which has been constantly growing since 1969. Relative to the total number of Jews in Sweden, the rate of aliyah is quite high.[15] The Chief Rabbi of the Stockholm community, Morton Narrowe, predicts that most of the devoted and involved Jews in Stockholm will leave, having accepted the belief that in order to survive as Jews, they must either live in Israel (where most of those who do emigrate go) or in America. Those who will not leave themselves are prepared to send their children away.[16] On the other hand, many leaders, especially in the smaller communities, fear the increasing interest in aliyah as a detriment to the continuation of Jewish life and leadership in Sweden and would like to see the young people remain within their communities.[17] Most recently there has been a slight increase in the emigration of professionals seeking employment elsewhere for lack of appropriate work in Sweden.

The Economic Basis of the Community

There are no official data on the economic structure of Sweden's Jews, but it appears that there is a great range of occupations and a strong tendency among the younger people to graduate from universities and enter the professions or the civil service. In the Stockholm area, the Jews follow the occupational trends common among Jews in the western world, rather than the trends within Sweden, with a preponderance in the fields of trade and services. A large percentage of Stockholm Jews are self-employed. The percentage of Jewish industrial workers in Stockholm, mainly post-1945 refugees, is low; however, the percentage of factory workers is higher in the smaller Jewish communities, which are often in industrial areas.[18]

As a result of the negative worldwide economic situation of the 1970's, many members of the Jewish communities have applied for a reduction in community tax assessment and some have left the communities altogether. Most who have left, however, had always been marginal Jews. Another consequence of the present economic situation is the growing number of academically trained Swedes who have emigrated or returned to universities for advanced degrees. In the Jewish community this has caused many university graduates, especially in Stockholm, to consider pursuing careers in Jewish professions. Many have turned to the local Jewish communities for financial assistance to study outside Scandinavia--usually in Israel.[19]

Intermarriage and Assimilation

There are no official statistics on the rate of intermarriage in Sweden; however, it is estimated that it is between 40 percent and 60 percent, a fact that is characteristic of all Scandinavian Jewish communities. Generally, in most of the cases where figures were recorded, the non-Jewish spouse converts, hence the actual rate may be much higher than official estimates. It is thought that there are over 10,000 individuals living in Sweden today that are either half, quarter, or one-eighth Jewish and who have completely integrated into Swedish society.[20] The high degree of intermarriage, both today and throughout Swedish Jewish history, reflects the relatively low degree of anti-Semitism in the country, the small proportion of Jews relative to the total population, and the pervasive feelings of relative liberalism and disassociation from religion. Couples of mixed marriage are accepted into Jewish communal life, and their children often attend the Hillel Jewish Day School. Non-Jewish spouses often participate in or show interest in Jewish organizations or in work for Israel, and Jewish spouses of mixed marriages are leaders of Jewish organizations.[21] Nevertheless, recent studies of Jewish identity indicate that perhaps 80 percent of Jews interviewed opposed intermarriage and almost half those Jews who were married to non-Jews were also against the practice.[22]

Anti-Semitism

Early anti-Semitism in Sweden was based on religious and economic attitudes and factors. In general, while Sweden is known for its liberalism, the Swedish people have demonstrated a certain xenophobia within their own borders.

In the period preceding World War II, Swedish Nazis, many paid by Germany, and other reactionary groups introduced smear campaigns and other attacks against the Jews. The Swedes, believing in free speech and press, did little to suppress anti-Semitic agitation. The Jewish community itself was divided in what course to take, most trying to use silence as a weapon, while the Zionists believed in bringing the issue out into the open. The battle was led by Daniel Brick, then representative of the Jewish Agency in Sweden and editor of the Judisk Kronika. Other Jewish leaders, notably Professor Hugo Valentin and Chief Rabbi Marcus Ehrenpreis, wrote pamphlets explaining anti-Semitism and lectures and radio programs were devoted to the subject. In the 1930 election the two fascist anti-Semitic groups in Sweden polled only 1.6 percent of the popular vote. Attempts were made by the Germans in 1938 to pressure Swedish business firms to dismiss Jewish employees, but they were met with stiff resistance. The church and press criticized the deportation of Norwegian Jews.

11

A new penal code came into effect in 1949,
stating that "to publicly slander or abuse any
individual or group of people of any race or faith
because of his or their racial origin or religious
belief" would be punishable by fine or imprisonment.
The law included a clause against injuring or
ridiculing the sacred objects or practices of a church
or acknowledged religious community.[23]

Nonetheless there have been several occurrences
of anti-Semitism since the 1950's, falling into
categories of anti-Semitic press, neo-Nazi acts
against Jews and attitudes of prejudice towards the
Jews. The following are examples of each category.

The synagogue in Göteborg was desecrated in 1952
and in 1959-1960 there were several acts of swastika
and slogan smearing throughout the country. These
acts were met by heavy criticism from the Swedish
government and people, even to raising the issue in
both houses of the Swedish Parliament. The Swedish
Minister of Justice claimed that the vandals who
committed these acts were drawn from among those
Swedish youth who found a lack of ideas and purpose in
Swedish society and who were influenced by the
world-wide publicity given to similar acts abroad at
that time.

Also in 1952, the World Jewish Congress called
upon the Swedish government to withdraw postal
facilities from anti-Semitic publishing firms alleged
to be the nucleus of an international anti-Semitic
organization. Two years later anti-Jewish literature
written by Einar Abery, one of Sweden's main
Jew-baiters, was sent to many American Senators and
Congressmen. There are two regular anti-Semitic
publications printed in Sweden: the Göteborg weekly
Fria Ord (successor to the Stockholm Dagsosten of the
Hitler era) and Nordisk Kamp, from Malmö. It is
believed that at least part of the funds for
subsidizing the papers have come from sources within
Sweden itself.[24] It is very difficult to curb the
anti-Semitic press in Sweden because of the nation's

liberal regulations regarding freedom of speech and press.

Swedish Nazis resumed their efforts to reestablish a neo-Nazi movement in Sweden in 1955, by founding student organizations at the universities of Uppsala, Stockholm and Lund. The groups unified under a central organization, the Swedish National Students' Federation, and affiliated to the Malmö section of the European Social Movement. In 1960, the Scandinavian National Party held a meeting at Stockholm Civic Hall, addressed by Jew-baiter Assar Oredson of Malmö. A Jewish Chronicle article in 1960 reported that Oredson's party numbered up to thousands, having branches in most of the bigger towns. In 1973, for the first time since World War II, Oredson's party ran in the general election.[25]

Two attitudinal studies of Swedish society also point to a lack of complete harmony between Jews and other Swedes. A survey taken in 1958 on the extent of racial prejudice in Sweden showed that 20 percent of the interviewees objected to working with Jews (8 percent in urban areas), 34 percent felt that Jews would cheat them in business, and 46 percent would try to dissuade their daughters from marrying Jews.[26] Another study was conducted in 1968 on the attitudes held by members of the Swedish Parliament on ethnic minorities and immigration. This study revealed that members of Parliament found it difficult to define the term "Jew" clearly, nearly 47 percent defining Jews as a race. While almost one-third agreed that Jewish children should have the right to attend Jewish day schools, more than 60 percent believed the Jews in Sweden should become assimilated into the rest of Swedish culture.[27]

The leading Swedish newspaper, Daily News, published two strongly pro-Arab articles in February 1974 in which it claimed that Israel had murdered Syrian civilians during the Yom Kippur War and the subsequent War of Attrition. One could separate Swedish attitudes about Israel from those about Jews more easily were it not for statements like the one

13

made by Oredson and his neo-Nazi party, claiming that their organization was not anti-Jewish but anti-Zionist.[28]

One can see that the seeds of political anti-Semitism seem to be growing within Swedish society, perhaps as a result of the growing popularity of the Swedish New Left political movements, which are strongly and vocally anti-Israel in nature. It is too early to judge clearly the degree of danger these movements represent for Swedish Jewry. However, the trend has become increasingly apparent since the Six Day War, and by 1973 the Stockholm Jewish community found it difficult to obtain a speaker from the Social Democratic Party to address the audience at Israel's twenty-fifth anniversary celebrations in Stockholm. The rise in aliyah from Sweden since 1969 can be partly attributed to the rebuff by and disappointment in the New Left felt by Swedish Jewish youth.[29]

Although, compared with other countries, Sweden has comparatively little anti-Semitism, it does exist, and has become stronger. Jewish children are often left with the feeling that they are, in fact, different from other Swedish children, even in their names. Since many in the community, especially in the old established families, have tried so hard to deny both their separate Jewish character and the presence of anti-Semitism, it might do well for the community to reassess the issue.

Jewish Identification

Schwarz's study of the Swedish Parliament's attitude toward Jews points out the psychological reactions of most Jews who immigrated to Sweden before 1945. Their strong desire to assimilate into the host culture historically took several forms: intermarriage and assimilation, nineteenth century adaptation of Jewish religious services to Christian-style worship, attempts at the turn of this century to halt East European migration, etc. Such

14

antagonism against other Jews reached its peak in the 1930's, with the Stockholm community's efforts to stem immigration.[30]

Creation of the State of Israel seems to have been a turning point in Jewish self-perception in Sweden. As identification with the Jewish State and world Jewry increased, Sweden's Jews began to develop a more organized Jewish life. Reparations payments enabled construction of many community facilities, but equally important was the gradual desire for a more intense Jewish life, generated mainly by the Second World War and post-war immigrants on the one hand, and some of the younger, native-born Swedes on the other. Preceding the Six Day War in 1967 a solidarity meeting for Israel was held at the Stockholm Community Synagogue. Many of the two thousand participants at the meeting had shown no prior interest in Jewish life.[31] Since the war, the Hillel Day School, membership in Bnei Akiva and other Jewish youth groups have all increased in scope and importance. Tourism to Israel and participation in a variety of volunteer schemes in Israel have also grown.

A case study in Malmö, conducted by Liva Herz in 1968, examined the attitudes of identification or assimilation among a sampling of forty younger (17-25 years old) and older (over 40) Swedish-born Jews and mostly Eastern European immigrants arriving after 1938. The study indicated that the majority of the older Swedish-born Jews interviewed conceive of themselves primarily as Swedes or as Swedes following the Jewish (Mosaic) religion, and explain their perception of their own Jewishness by the fact that they were born Jews and were used to following certain family traditions. This indicated that native-born Swedes identify with the majority group. The circle of friends among the group of native-born Swedes interviewed were mostly mixed or non-Jewish, expressing the group's desire to assimilate, rather than isolate itself among the Jewish community. Older Swedish-born Jews were active in Jewish organizations, seeing such affiliation as their responsibility to prevent Jewish culture from disappearing and in order to help other Jews.

The younger Swedish-born Jews showed a different identification pattern. They felt that Judaism represented a peoplehood as well as a religion. One of the factors in determining their identification seems to be periods of residence or travel in Israel, as well as mixing with young Jewish immigrants in Sweden. The young Swedes interviewed identified more frequently with other Jews than did their immigrant contemporaries, indicating that perhaps young Swedes were more in need of having Jewish friends in order to maintain or reinforce their Jewish identification, especially if they came from homes in which Judaism did not play a large role in their lives.

The immigrant groups interviewed for the study showed a strong identification with the national element in Jewishness, perhaps reflecting the negative experiences they endured at the hands of non-Jews in their homelands and perhaps as a result of the more intense Jewish communal life of which they had been a part before immigrating to Sweden. Most older immigrants tended to perpetuate friendship groups among their own circles, feeling a common denominator binding them and other immigrants, because of their past experiences and hardships in assimilating in Sweden, and being conscious that their accents labeled them as foreigners. The young immigrants, however, had very mixed friendship circles.

All three groups, young native-born Swedes, young immigrants and older immigrants, belonged to Jewish organizations as expressions of their group consciousness and identification, and all four groups generally opposed intermarriage.[32]

In the past twenty years a trend has grown toward outward expression of Jewishness and a desire to explain it to non-Jews. In 1957 the Institute for Jewish Culture and Information was opened in Stockholm. Its aims are to promote understanding of Judaism, Jewish history, and Zionism among both Jews and Christians, to combat racial prejudice and foster intergroup understanding. More recently, influenced greatly by the Polish-Jewish immigration, there is a return to Yiddish and Hebrew, as well as a desire to study about Judaism at a serious level. A Judaica library has been opened in Lund and plans are now underway, headed by an interreligious committee of professors called the Judaica Research Society, to establish a faculty of Judaica at one of the Swedish universities.

At the same time, approximately one-third of the Jews in Stockholm are not formally affiliated with the community. There are three main reasons for non-affiliation. To many, especially in the Jewish scientific community, affiliation with a "religious" community would be an act of hypocrisy. Like other communities, the Jewish community was founded and recognized as a religious community to accommodate the new nationalism of nineteenth century Europe which allowed religious pluralism but discouraged other forms. Since it remains officially a religious body, many intellectual atheists and agnostics feel the necessity to act as dissenters and not participate in the community. However, the establishment of the State of Israel has enabled many of this group to express their Jewish identification in other ways: deep contacts have been established with colleagues working in Israeli scientific fields, frequent trips and work visits take place, contributions to Israel fund-raising drives are made, and so on.

A second reason for lack of affiliation with the community follows a process seen in other countries, where many survivors of the Holocaust attempt to deny their identification, hoping in this way perhaps to blot out their memories, or perhaps seeking to take revenge on their Jewishness, which in the past caused them so much suffering. In Sweden, this act of protest is paralleled by those who accuse the Jewish community of withholding full support for Jewish immigration in the early years of the war and for failing to integrate the immigrants socially into Jewish communal life.

17

The third reason for non-affiliation with the community is a practical rather than an ideological one. Membership in the Stockholm community is financed by a 2.4 percent tax levied bi-monthly on all members. Since it is possible to receive some social benefits from the community regardless of membership, many people see no need to formally join. Yet, most Jews, and a great percentage of those who are only part Jewish, attend Jewish rallies, special meetings and celebrations and contribute to Israeli causes.[33]

The Structure of the Swedish Jewish Community

The following centers of Jewish population are united under the Central Council of Swedish Jewish Communities: Stockholm, Mälmo, Göteborg, Nörrkoping, Boras, Örebro, Hälsingborg, Karlstaad, Kalmar, Sundsvall, Eskiltuna, Vasteras, Kristianstad, Council are the elected heads of the three main communities (Stockholm, Mälmo and Göteborg) and some of the smaller ones. Although the Central Council meets only when there is a specific issue to discuss, by virtue of the fact that it does meet together to solve problems that arise, it may be considered a policy-making body. Issues discussed range from problems of kosher slaughtering to the continuity of Jewish life in the smaller communities. For daily affairs, however, the Stockhold Jewish Community is regarded as the spokesman for Swedish Jewry. Often the Stockholm Community officially includes the Central Council in honorary obligations (such as formal salutations to the Government of Sweden or in the ceremonials relating to Israeli government officials).[35]

The three major local communities act as metropolitan service centers for many of the smaller ones. The Jewish Community of Stockholm also serves Jews in the following smaller towns: Nörrkoping, Örebro, Kalmar, Sundsvall, Eskilstuna, Vasteras, Uppsala, Karlstaad, Sodertalje; the Jewish Community of Mälmo serves the communities of Landskrona, Halmstad, Hälsingbord, Kristianstad, and Lund; and the Jewish Community of Göteborg serves the Jews in Boras.[36] Generally the needs of Jews in the small communities are not financial, since social services are so highly developed in Sweden, but are rather, educational, cultural, religious and organizational. The larger communities send lecturers, teachers and rabbis and engage in limited youth work for the smaller communities.[37] Members of the smaller communities serve on committees of the larger communities, especially in Stockholm. Relief work still conducted by the Jewish community is coordinated among the three large communities, with two smaller ones providing aid to the needy in their geographical areas. Grants for social work benefitting victims of the Nazis have been brought about through the Stockholm Community and have been directly appropriated to the Communities in Göteborg and Mälmo.[38]

The Zionist Federation of Sweden is the most dynamic country-wide organization in the Swedish Jewish community. As of 1975, approximately one thousand Jews belonged to the Zionist Federation directly and another two thousand were members of subsidiary organizations (WIZO, various Zionist parties, Keren Kayemet le Israel, Keren Hayesod, Bnei Akiva, Habonim, Makabbi).[39]

The Zionist Federation is directed by a twenty-one member National Board, seventeen members representing various groups in Stockholm and four members representing groups in other cities. The National Board is elected by the Conference of the Zionist Federation, usually held bi-annually. The National Board, in turn, elects a six member Executive.[40]

As a response to growing Swedish support of the Palestinians and of growing threats of anti-Semitism folowing the Six Day War, the Stockholm Community and the Zionist Federation organized the Solidarity Committee for Israel, composed of representatives from the Community and from the Zionist Federation in equal proportions. A professional journalist was hired to serve as full-time director of the committee, but for all intents and purposes it is run by the Zionist Federation. The committee disseminates information on Israel and Judaism through news reviews, a telephone center, press conferences, and the organization of smaller action committees. The Solidarity Committee is a Jewish body but it has close contact with the

Youth Group for Peace in the Middle East, an organization three-fourths of whose members are non-Jews, which works in schools and campuses throughout the country.[41] Similar Solidarity Committees operate in the other large communities.

Two country-wide organizations are comprised mainly of non-Jews, although their initiative and professional aid comes from the Jewish community and the Zionist Federation. The Swedish-Israel Friendship Leagues are comprised mainly of prominent non-Jewish politicians and academicians. The Swedish Friends of the Kibbutz send people in goodly numbers (mostly non-Jews) to work temporarily in kibbutzim.[42]

The Organization of 45'ers has local branches in several Swedish communities. Comprised of post World War II refugees, the organization was useful in obtaining German reparations which built many Jewish communal buildings, especially in Malmö where the organization is still very strong. There has been conflict in that community between the 45'ers and the Zionist Federation, which represents younger native-born or more culturally assimilated Jews.

B'nai Brith is a very respected and active organization in Sweden. The first lodge was established in Stockholm in 1949, with lodges in Malmö and Göteborg being formed soon after. B'nai Brith is the only Jewish secular group in Stockholm that meets exclusively at its own headquarters. As in other chapters, Swedish B'nai Brith activities include cultural events, lectures and social activities. An effort is consciously made in planning activities to increase members' knowledge about all things Jewish; in addition it deals with secular humanitarian problems.[43] Swedish B'nai Brith works closely with other Scandinavian B'nai Brith lodges and the Scandinavian B'nai Brith Council.

Jewish students in Sweden are structurally united under two umbrella organizations: the Nordic Jewish Students Association (NOIS) and the Scandinavian Jewish Youth Federation (SJUC), of which NOIS is an

21

affiliate.[44] It was estimated that in 1972, one thousand Jewish students were studying in Swedish universities -- about three hundred in Stockholm, fifty in Uppsala and between four hundred and five hundred in Lund. In the ensuing years, Jewish enrollment decreased, having passed the peak of the post World War II "baby boom" children of university age, but many young adults have either continued their studies or begun them recently because of the difficulties in the labor market.

The Jewish Community of Stockholm

The Jewish Community of Stockholm (Mosaiska Formsalingen i Stockholm), representing between 7,000 and 8,000 Jews living in the area, is the largest and most powerful Community in the country, and represents Swedish Jewry in dealings with national and international organizations, Jewish and non-Jewish. As of 1968, approximately 5,000, or two-thirds of the Jewish residents in greater Stockholm and the surrounding districts, were affiliated with the Community.[45]

Governance of the Community is in the hands of a twenty-five member Board of Deputies, elected every three years, following the Swedish electoral cycle. The deputies in turn appoint a board of seven administrators, five of whom are responsible for specific communal functions. All members in good standing of the Community are entitled to vote, and about two thousand actually do so.[46]

The Jewish Community of Stockholm deals with most aspects of Jewish life and undertakes all activities concerning the Jewish population in general in the country. Thus it is the center of social, cultural and religious work affecting the Stockholm Jewish community and all of Swedish Jewry.

The Stockholm Jewish Center was initiated in 1963 under a grant from the Joint Distribution Committee.

It is a community center in the best sense, a meeting place widely used by groups and individuals alike. Study circles, the Hillel School and Community Kindergarten, Bnei Akiva, Habonim, SJUF (Jewish Youth Society for 15-18 year olds), the New Jewish Society (a social group for youth over the age of 18), the University of Stockholm Student Club, IK Makkabi, Club Babel, Keren Kayemet, WIZO, Keren Hayesod, the Zionist Federation, and other activities and organizations schedule large meetings in the Center hall or in permanent facilities assigned to the organizations. Membership at the Center is on a dues paying basis. In the last few years, efforts have been successfully made to involve young people in the regular activities of the Center. The Stockholm Community has a fine Judaica library, called the Bialik Library, which is housed at the Center and which sends exhibitions throughout the country.[47]

Organized Jewish life exists in a number of communities outside of Stockholm, as previously indicated. Distances restrict the frequency of contacts between Jews in the various settlements. As has been pointed out earlier, Swedes living in small provincial settlements tend to be more parochial with regard to non-conformists and sometimes are more anti-Semitic than their urban counterparts. With the lack of social contacts among their own people and a rather passive dislike of them as foreigners among the host community, many provincial Jews are losing their identification with Judaism and are attempting to integrate into Swedish life. In at least one case on record, old people meeting together as a Jewish group expressed their doubts as to who they were, why they should meet, or what form or content, if any, to give to their lives as Jews. However, many wished to have their children's ties to Israel and to Judaism strengthened. The youngsters also seemed to want to participate in an upsurge of Jewish and Zionist identification. It has been explained that the positive feelings they expressed might be a reaction to the general spiritual vacuum in Sweden. However, Sweden is lacking in young dynamic leadership to lead and teach in the small communities.[48]

23

Boras

Boras is a community of about 350-450 Jews, primarily Yiddish speaking World War II refugees. It is about a two hour drive from Göteborg. WIZO and the Zionist Federation have groups here and the community has a well-furnished Community Center.

Eskilstuna

The community, located approximately one hundred kilometers from Stockholm, has about thirty adult members. The Community Center houses most Jewish activities, which include religious services for the High Holidays, WIZO activities, a religious school which meets once a week, observances of the Warsaw ghetto uprising, and various cultural activities.[49]

Göteborg

Göteborg is the second largest city in Sweden and also has the second largest Jewish community. The first Jewish community here began in 1729 and was reestablished in 1780. It has had a Liberal (Reform) majority for many years. The community's Great Synagogue, considered the most beautiful in Sweden, celebrated its 120th anniversary in 1972. A Community Center was dedicated in 1962, with funds acquired from the Claims Conference, the Swedish government, local fund raising and loans. As is the pattern in Sweden, the Center houses sports and recreation rooms, a prayer room for the Orthodox congregation, local community offices, a large club room for the youth association and classrooms for the religious school. There is a kosher restaurant and a community library. Among the Jewish organizations operating in the community are WIZO, Bnei Akiva, B'nai Brith, Keren Kayemet and the Zionist Federation.

Affairs of the community are handled by a five member Board of Directors, elected directly by an assembly where each community member has voting privileges. In practice, about one hundred people attend these meetings. The first woman was elected to the Board of Directors in 1962, the first time a woman ever held such a post in the Swedish Jewish community.[50]

In the past three years youth work in Göteborg has become much more intensive. Together with the AJDC, the Youth and Hechalutz Department of the Jewish Agency began working with local and Polish Jewish immigrant youth. An Israeli student shaliach was sent to Göteborg to identify potential local leaders. The community has been receptive to these efforts and now finances the youth work. It provided a local Jewish student with a scholarship for study in the Hebrew University School of Social Work and then hired the graduate as full time youth leader at the center upon his return. There are three basic youth clubs in Göteborg: the Jewish Youth and Student Club, with a combined membership of 250 members, aged nine through eighteen; Hakoach Sports Club; and Bnei Akiva.

Göteborg has a Jewish day school for grades one through six and a religious school program for other students, which has recently taken the form of weekend camps and seminars organized by one of the day school teachers.[51]

About 150 Jewish students, most of Polish origin, study at the University of Göteborg and at the Institute of Technology.

Kristianstad

Between ten and fifteen Jewish families (about thirty persons) remain in Kristianstad out of a general population of just under 30,000. About fifteen years ago the community had an active organizational life; the newest synagogue in Sweden,

25

built in 1960, was built here. But today, as in many other small Swedish communities, the youth have left the town and many activities have ceased. WIZO still has a local chapter and several people belong to the B'nai Brith lodge in Malmö. Jews in Kristianstad pay membership dues to the Malmö Jewish Community. Religious services are still held each Sabbath, with practically all Jewish males in attendance, so that a minyan may be constituted. Most of the community keeps some form of kashrut at home. Hebrew classes are run by the community, with help from Malmö; classes have been held in public schools as well as in the synagogue. Unlike most small Swedish communities, the Jewish community of Kristianstad manifests a strong individual and communal sense of Jewishness. There is very little intermarriage in the community.[52]

Lund

About ten Jewish families live in Lund, but there are hundreds of Jewish students attending the university there, mostly post-1968 refugees from Poland. In 1971 the Jewish Agency sent a shaliach to work with the Jewish Students Club in Lund. Most of his efforts centered around integrating the Polish Jewish students into the rest of the Jewish student community. Since 1974 Israeli shlichim have been replaced by a Polish-born student living in Sweden who was trained for the work in Israel. In addition to his post as Youth Leader in Lund, he works with youth clubs in Malmö and Halsingborg. The Lund Jewish Student Club meets in a rented apartment that has been turned into a Jewish Student Center. There is also an old syngogue in Lund that is occasionally used.[53]

Malmö

Malmö is a very active Jewish community, but a very problematic one as well. The Jewish community numbers about 1,400 registered members, with probably

26

another one thousand new Polish immigrants who are unaffiliated. Most of the Jewish inhabitants of the city immigrated from Poland after 1945, so that the presence of older Swedish Jews is hardly felt. Most Jewish activity takes place at the Center, which is full nightly, with young and old alike. Nevertheless, there seems to be an apparent generation gap in the community: the older generation clings to Yiddish and the communal pattern of Jewish life reminiscent of Poland, while the younger generation finds that pattern lacking in meaning. Many of the young people belong to Bnei Akiva and are planning aliyah as an immediate solution to their Jewish problem in Sweden. By their emigration, they are causing a thinning out of leadership potential for the local Jewish community in general. Many of the Jews who remain seem to be drifting farther away from the community, although they continue to pay community taxes.

Expression of the growing dichotomy in the community can be shown in the pattern of affiliation with the local Jewish organizations. The Survivors of 1945, a largely Yiddish-speaking group, numbers about 220 members and is a well run organization. Most Swedish-born young families in the community identify more with the Swedish-speaking leadership of the local Zionist organization than with the Survivors' group, even though the Survivors' group is better organized. Friction between the two groups is considerable, representative of the general conflict between the Swedish-born and Polish-born Jews in the community. In 1963, the Community considered action to prevent Jews who had not paid Community taxes from participating in any Jewish communal activities. The proposal was, however, never adopted.

Köping

The community, about 150 kilometers from Stockholm, has a Jewish community of approximately twenty-five, some of whom are intermarried. It is very active in Zionist and pro-Israel affairs.

27

Nörrkoping

About 170 kilometers from Stockholm, this industrial community has about thirty Jewish families, ten of whom are part of an earlier large community which left a beautiful synagogue consecrated in 1858. The rest of the community are post-1968 immigrants from Poland, and the communal life of the group is Yiddishist.

Uppsala

Efforts are being made to integrate the Polish refugees and native-born Jews, but without too much success. A Jewish Student Club is active, a youth club has just been purchased, and a youth leader hired.

Vasteras

Vasteras has several organizations, with a fair amount of cooperation and support among them. Organizations include: WIZO, the Swedish-Israel Society, the Community and Keren Kayemet. Religious services are held on the holidays.[54]

Functions of the Swedish Jewish Community

Religious Needs

The majority os the Stockholm Community are what would be considered "Reform" or "Conservative" in the United States. The present Head Rabbi of the Stockholm Community is a graduate of The Jewish Theological Seminary of America (Conservative). The Main Synagogue of the Community holds Ashkenazic services, has separate seating but a mixed choir and organ, and uses a Conservative style prayerbook.[55] In addition to the mainstream congregation, there are two small Orthodox synagogues that are considered part of the Community: Yeshurun and Adath Israel, with a combined membership of approximately two hundred families. An Orthodox rabbi imported in 1973 by the Jewish Agency currently serves both congregations. At present his salary is paid by the synagogues, but negotiations are now underway to have the Community pay it directly, instead of the present practice of giving large subsidies to the synagogues.

It is estimated that less than two hundred Jews in Stockholm attend Sabbath services regularly. During the week, morning services are held twice weekly at the Main Synagogue (using traditional ritual) and an attempt is made to have a daily minyan in the Orthodox synagogues, with a generously estimated total for all services of approximately sixty. Attendance is higher on Jewish holidays and on the High Holidays the synagogues are full. Special youth services are arranged at various times and led by the different youth groups, often providing the rare occasion for youth to participate in formal worship.[56]

In addition to the two rabbis in Stockholm, there are two other rabbis in Sweden, a liberal rabbi in

Göteborg and a traditional one in Malmö. All belong to the Conference of Scandinavian Rabbis.

The Women's League of the Stockholm Community serves the same functions for the Main Synagogue as any synagogue sisterhood in the United States. Classes in Bible and Talmud are offered in the Orthodox synagogues, as well as in a Bnei Akiva study group, but all are on a limited scale.[57]

The ritual slaughtering of meat is a serious problem in Sweden, where laws forbid the regular shechita process. Sometime following World War II special permission was granted the community by the Chief Ashkenazic Rabbi of Jerusalem, by which the precise time of slaughter could be timed to correspond with an electric shock that stunned the animal, thus making the slaughter acceptable to the authorities. However, this is a complicated process, requiring good supervision, and most of the Orthodox community in Sweden do not accept the compromise, especially after the Chief Rabbi of Israel some years ago also questioned its acceptability, and import their meat from Denmark. Now, the Central Council of Jewish Communities in Sweden is discussing the possibility of opening new slaughterhouses throughout the country, in addition to the central one outside Malmö.[58]

The Stockholm community will soon have a mikvah for the first time in many years, through private contributions. However, at present the demand for one is very small.[59]

The Stockholm Jewish Community maintains four Jewish cemeteries, two of which are still in use. There are different fees for purchase of cemetary plots, depending on the length of time one has been a member of the Community. Burial arrangements are directed by the Jewish Sick Aid and Burial Society, which also supplies a community nurse and doctor. In 1973, the association arranged eighty-eight burials at the Community cemeteries.[60] Burial privileges continue to be a primary incentive to retain

30

membership in the Stockholm Jewish Community, as in other communities throughout the country.

The Committee for the Promotion of Religious Needs, a sub-committee of the Second Social Section of the Board of Deputies of the Community, directs the religious facilities in Stockholm suburbs and in outlying provincial communities, by arranging holiday worship services, providing support to families in order to maintain kosher homes, supplying matzot, prayerbooks and other religious articles when necessary, and supporting the maintenance of the mikvah. The committee is involved in directing a translation of the Pentateuch and haftarot into Swedish.[61]

Social Services

Social services in the Stockholm community are supplied through the First and Second Social Sections of the Board of Deputies of the Community.[62]

The first Social Section coordinates aid given to needy families that arrived in Sweden before 1945. This group is much smaller than the group that arrived later and its budget is small.

The Second Social Section seems to be by far the most important of the Community's committees. The Section is comprised of the Chairman of the Community, the rabbi, and eleven members elected by the Community delegation. Some are representatives of the Association of Nazi Victims in Sweden. The task of this committee was originally to aid immigrants from Nazi persecution in social, relief and cultural matters. Since 1945, and especially in view of the immigration from Hungary and Poland, the committee's mandate has been extended to serve all refugees arriving after World War II.

Subcommittees under the direction of the Second Social Section include: social, scholarship, loan,

31

promotion of religious needs, cultural, and the United Restitution Organization.

The Social Committee was given new functions with the Hungarian and Polish immigrations. In recent years most recipients of relief have been invalids, families in which the breadwinner has reduced working capacity, and elderly persons in poor financial circumstances, as well as people needing temporary assistance only. The Section commissioned a study of its services by a university lecturer, assisted by the Welfare officers of the City of Stockholm Family Advice Bureau. Sweden provides social insurance benefits and the Second Social Section attempts to assist its clients in obtaining them. However, it is not always possible to do so, and large expenditures of the Community are used to supplement or replace those benefits. In addition, agreements with West Germany provided compensation for former Danish and Norwegian concentration camp prisoners and to parents, widows, and children of victims of the Nazis.

Care of the aged falls under the guidance of the Second Social Section. The Jewish Nursing Home for Chronic Invalids in Stockholm was opened in 1959. There is also a Home for Jewish Pensioners in Stockholm, built in 1945 and recently remodeled. The combined number of residents in the two institutions is approximately sixty. The Second Section helps defray costs, but the institutions are largely self-supporting. Any member of the community is eligible for admittance to either institution and application is made directly to the Community office. Following the general trend in Sweden, the community tries to maintain old people in their own homes for as long as possible, so arrangements are made to help the aged with their domestic requirements. The Jewish Women's League provides a great deal of assistance in this matter.[63]

The scholarship committee was established in 1946. Its work is carried out by a trained social worker. In addition to economic aid, counseling regarding studies and information concerning

32

scholarships for retraining is given. Scholarships are provided for study in universities, commercial schools, technical colleges, nursing and medical schools, artistic professions and Jewish studies. Orientation is given as to the possibilities of obtaining scholarships from public organizations, from ordinary school funds of the community and the Israelite Young Men's Fund. In 1972, fifty-six scholarships were granted by this committee and from other funds. Of the recipients, twenty-one were new immigrants.[64]

The loan committee was initially set up in 1955 with an allocation from the Claims Conference, and has been supported by both that body and the community. The committee's aim is to aid refugees in setting themselves up in private businesses. In the period from its inception to 1960 approximately 104 loans had been awarded.

Generally speaking, the number of people aided by the Second Social Section is diminishing through death, and the social services are being slowly reduced accordingly, or replaced by new services to the Polish Jewish immigrants.[65]

The United Restitution Organization in Stockholm deals with individual compensation claims according to West German laws of restitution for Nazi victims. Until the end of 1973, 2,097 persons had received about 132.5 million crowns. These numbers include those persons who were able to leave Eastern Europe after 1953 and before 1966. There are about two hundred persons in this category. The number of persons receiving life annuities because of damages to health, professions, or close relatives was 1,135 at the end of 1972.[66]

Culture

The Cultural Committee of the Community places increasing stress on the importance of education and

33

the building up of youth activities among groups in the provinces, as well as in maintaining cultural ties among the adults. In 1964, ten clubs, with a total of 550 adult members received financial support from the Community.[67] It is assumed that the number has considerably increased since then. Since 1972, representatives of the new Polish immigrants have turned to the Cultural Committee for assistance in establishing and implementing a Jewishly centered cultural program for their group. They are now directly represented on the committee, an important innovation in communal life.

The work of the Cultural Committee is handled by three subcommittees: work in the provinces and all general cultural work in Stockholm, work with the Polish immigrants -- adults and youngsters, and the Bialik library. The committee has recently established a Yiddish theater and supports the newly founded Society for Judaic Research. However, the financial means available to the Cultural Committee are minimal and make it extremely difficult to make a serious kind of contribution.[68]

In the educational sphere, the committee arranges for religious teaching in eleven locations in the provinces. During 1972, eighteen pupils in the four provincial settlements of Eskilstuna, Köping, Södertalje and Uppsala received class instruction; a teacher "circuit rides" to other towns. Provincial education in the Stockholm district falls under the supervision of the Stockholm Community's School Board. In addition to the support given to the provinces' clubs' junior sections, totalling about 240 young people, the committee helps organize young adult seminars and winter camps for Swedish Jewish youth. It is expected that responsibility for instruction in new settlements will probably rest in the hands of the large communities, especially that of Stockholm, for a long time, but work in other respects among the new groups will probably depend largely on the degree of responsibility taken among the group members themselves.[69]

A study of Jewish education in the Diaspora was compiled by the World Zionist Organization in 1971. It showed that approximately 50 percent of Swedish children received some form of Jewish education in 1967, one hundred in the day school and 1,300 in supplementary classes.[70]

When the Hillel School was founded in 1955, it precipitated a crisis in the community. Strong debates centered around the issue of whether establishing a Jewish day school was tantamount to ghettoization or not. Most of the Community leadership, following the Liberal Jewish Forum trend (Reform Judaism), espoused integration of the Jewish population within Swedish society and saw the formation of a Jewish school as an obstacle to achieving this goal. However, many post-1945 refugees, who themselves had come from more intensive Jewish life in Eastern Europe, demanded a more traditional and more Zionist education for their children. Thus the Society Forenigen Chinuch was founded in the early 1950's. Although a separate entity from the Zionist Federation, many of its leaders came from the Zionist group. A special subsidy from the Claims Conference and a fund raising campaign within the community raised the initial money for the school. Tuition fees are set according to the parents' income, and, in addition, allocations to the school are made by the Claims Conference and the Community (the latter subsidy covering the religious instruction and the Jewish history program). Aid is also given by the State, an unusual phenomenon in light of its usual refusal to encourage pluralism.[71]

In 1963, when the Jewish Center of Stockholm was inaugurated, facilities were provided on its premises for the Hillel School, thus encouraging the children to utilize the Center's other facilities and take part in its other activities as well. Today, approximately 125 children are studying in grades one through six. In addition to a full public school program, an intensive Jewish, but not Orthodox, education is provided, with a Zionist orientation, presented by

Israeli teachers and adhering to an Israel-centered curriculum.

The controversy over the dangers of ghettoization resulting from the school's existence has diminished and now it is possible to find children of many former critics attending the school, because of its high standard of achievement.[72] Attempts have been made to extend the course of study through ninth grade but there are not enough students to allow for the type of varied curriculum junior high schools offer. Instead, through the efforts of the Forenigen Chinuch, one of the secondary schools in Stockholm offers credit courses in Jewish studies for Hillel School graduates.[73]

The Community maintains a nursery school and kindergarten, founded in 1952 by the Forenigen Chinuch, also at the Jewish Center building. Approximately forty to fifty children attend the school. Much of the nursery's budget is provided by the Nachmansonska Foundation, a Community finance committee which also supports the summer camps and other schools and youth work. The Community contributes to the budget as well.[74]

A special Religious School Committee of the Community directs the educational work of a one-day-a-week religious school for the Stockholm area. As of 1972, a total of 213 students were enrolled in the school, in classes ranging from grades two through twelve. No financial aid is given the school by the government, since it is entirely supplementary to the regular educational curriculum. Most of the classes meet at the Community Center. Very little can actually be taught in a one-hour-a-week curriculum, but an attempt is made to foster some sort of appreciation of history and customs. For most Stockholm youth, this is the maximum Jewish education received, and the only instruction offered past the sixth grade. However, an increasingly popular approach to the education of teenagers is the "Shabbat seminar" or retreat, held periodically at Glämsta campsite by the Religious

Committee and the rabbis, and occasional Shabbat morning get-togethers in the city. A combined Bar-Mitzvah and Bat-Mitzvah group is active and plans have been made for study seminars for fifteen and sixteen year olds to be held in Israel upon completion of a preparatory course in Sweden.[75]

In 1970, the Swedish Ministry of Education replaced its compulsory Christian Religion Course (from which Jews and Moslems were exempt upon proof of study in their own religion classes) with units on Comparative Religion, taught as an integral part of the history curriculum. Attendance at the Jewish studies classes has not seemed to dwindle with this change in curriculum; children (and/or their parents) who chose some form of Jewish education before did so because of a desire to identify with the Jewish community and not as an excuse not to study Christianity.[76]

One of the problems in Jewish education was the lack of Jewish textbooks in Swedish. The Hillel Publishing House, connected with the Community and the Forenigen Chinuch, has published a collection of short stories for children and a children's book about post-biblical Jewish leaders, with more books and translations in process. Several textbooks have already been translated from English. The Community hopes to spread the books throughout the Swedish school system, making them available in libraries and as supplemental aids to teachers in the lower and junior high grades. Many schools showed an interest in learning about Judaism and the Swedish Jewish community as a result of good publicity about the bicentennial of Jewish settlement in Sweden which took place in 1975.

Apart from the education provided for children living outside Stockholm under the direction of the Second Social Section, as previously described, the Nachmansonska Foundation of the Stockholm Community provides special grants to the Jewish nursery schools in Göteborg and Malmö.

The Stockholm Community conducts a summer camp, called Glämsta, at a permanent camp-site near Stockholm. Two three-week sessions are held for children nine through fifteen, in which Jewish studies, Hebrew, and religious observances are part of the camp program. In 1972, 190 children attended the camp, coming from Stockholm, Göteborg, Mälmo, and several smaller communities throughout the country. For several years the Community also conducted a Jewish Studies Institute near Nörrkoping for children living outside the Community's sphere of activities. The Institute was closed in 1966.[78]

From 1968 until 1972 selected youngsters and young adults were sent to the Ramah summer camps in the United States or participated in the Ramah program in Israel.[79] All Ramah programs in the United States and in Israel are run by the American Conservative movement. Perhaps the most successful camps are those of the Scandinavian Bnei Akiva movement. Rather than use a permanent campsite, the camp is held each year at different locations in Scandinavia, mostly in Sweden. Youngsters also participate in other Bnei Akiva camps throughout Europe. The Scandinavian Youth Organization holds three camps annually--two for teenagers and one for young adults.

Youth

A strong emphasis is placed on youth work in the Jewish community of Sweden, both in Stockholm itself and in the outlying communities. In addition to the educational and summer camping programs initiated by the Stockholm Community and financial help given through its Second Social Section, direct aid is given to major youth organizations in the form of facilities and leadership assistance. Social contact is a goal in itself in such a small community so open to social assimilation. Thus one sees parents who may not themselves be active in Jewish life encouraging their children to participate in Jewish youth groups, especially in the smaller communities.

As is true in the general Swedish community, the affluence and security provided by the social-state fostered under the "Swedish experiment" is felt by many to have left a void in the aspirations of youth who lack ideals for which to strive. Jewish youth, however, still have the ideal of Zionism to attain, as well as of defending the rights and strengthening ties between world Jewry. Consequently, a high percentage of Swedish Jewish youth are active at various community centers and proportionately, aliyah from Sweden is high.[80] Particularly since the Six Day War, young Jews in Sweden have been reexamining their commitment to Judaism and the Jewish people.

The Youth and Hechalutz Department of the Jewish Agency, through its British Desk, has taken the lead in developing and sustaining youth activities. The department has three shlichim working in the large communities and frequently traveling to the smaller ones. All Jewish Agency subsidies are passed through the senior shaliach in Stockholm and are granted for specific activities rather than as direct subventions to the organizations. The Youth and Hechalutz Department has trebled its activities in Scandinavia in the past three years. The Youth and Hechalutz Department has succeeded in attracting a number of native-born and Polish Jewish young adults to communal work. The deputy director of the Stockholm Jewish Community Center, the youth leader in Malmö and head of the Pedagogic and Resource Center and youth leader in Lund and Malmö were trained through that department.[81]

Bnei Akiva

Bnei Akiva is the largest Zionist youth movement in Sweden. The office of the Scandinavian shaliach to Bnei Akiva rotates between Copenhagen and Stockholm and is presently situated in Stockholm. Although Bnei Akiva is a religious movement, many of its Swedish, indeed, Scandinavian members in general, are often religious only for the time they are in the movement and sometimes only while attending Bnei Akiva activities. Parents greatly encourage membership, although they are not themselves religious. The Stockholm branch has approximately 150 members; approximately twenty-five are active in Göteborg and approximately thirty-five in Malmö. However, many more youngsters participate in Scandinavian Bnei Akiva camps and seminars.[82]

Habonim

Habonim is the only non-Orthodox Zionist youth movement in existence in Sweden. Active only in Stockholm, Habonim has between forty and sixty members. Like Bnei Akiva, Habonim headquarters are at the Stockholm Jewish Community Center. Since 1974, the Youth and Hechalutz Department hired an Israeli student at the University of Stockholm to work as part-time leader for the group. The Habonim Executive is composed of local members. Occasionally weekend seminars are held in Sweden, but more often members participate in camps and seminars run by Habonim in England or Holland.[83]

I.K. Makkabi

Makkabi Sports Club is an active organization in Stockholm, with a membership of about five hundred youngsters and adults. Its activities follow the full gamut of sports and gymnastics. Makkabi is connected with the Swedish Sports Society and World Makkabi. It has its own sports center but uses the Jewish Community Center's facilities whenever feasible. In 1976 Makkabi became a member of the World Zionist Organization.[84]

40

Club Babel

On March 25, 1972 a new clubroom was opened at the Jewish Center in Stockholm, for about one hundred young people, aged 17-25, children of post-1968 immigrants from Poland. Aims of the club are to foster a stronger relationship to Judaism and Israel. At first the Center leaders wanted to incorporate the Polish youngsters into already existing youth clubs, but the need was recognized for a group of their own, from which they could then integrate into other Center activities at their own speed. The Joint Distribution Committee and the Community share operating expenses of the group. Activities include evenings of lectures and discussions, meetings with young immigrants living in the provinces, courses in Jewish history and religion, camping seminars and combined activities with other clubs at the Center. The leadership of the club has already begun to take an active part in other community activities and serves as a catalyst for other youth groups.[85]

SJUF and NOIS

In Sweden, SJUF chapters exist in Stockholm (approximately three hundred members in 1972), Uppsala (approximately thirty members), and Lund (approximately one hundred paying members). Swedish SJUF is an auxiliary member of the Stockholm Community.[86]

NOIS, the Scandinavian Union of Jewish Students, has branches in Stockholm, Uppsala, Lund, and Göteborg, as well as in Helsinki, Oslo, Trondheim, and Copenhagen. The present chairman of NOIS, son of a family of Jewish leaders, is from Stockholm. Most of the Jewish student activists in NOIS are Polish Jews. NOIS organizes its own seminars for Scandinavian Jewish students. Because of the limited size of membership, one sees the same participants at most seminars, whether called by NOIS, SJUF, or WUJS.[87]

Zionist Activities

The Limit Federation

The Zionist Federation of Sweden is the most
dynamic country-wide organization in the Swedish
Jewish community. Until World War II, Zionism played
a small role in determining the character of communal
life, an understandable fact in light of the Reform
and assimilationist-oriented tendencies of the Swedish
Jewish population.

However, the marked increase of East Europeans
following World War II introduced a highly Zionist-
oriented group into the community, whose desire to
foster a more intensive Jewish life included
a strong commitment to the Zionist cause. The
organizational background and commitment of the
Eastern Europeans had allowed them to practice their
leadership skills within the Swedish community, and
already in the post-war years, the Zionist movement
assumed a major role in Jewish life.[88]

As of 1975, approximately one thousand Jews
belonged to the Zionist Federation directly and
another two thousand were members of auxiliary
organizations (WIZO, various parties, Keren Kayemet le
Israel, Keren Hayesod, Bnei Akiva, Habonim). Except
for WIZO, which will be discussed separately,
all the different party factions and organizations
within the Zionist Federation become active only
during election campaigns to the World Zionist
Congresses. Otherwise, all Zionist Federation
activities are combined.

The Swedish Zionist Federation takes charge of
local Zionist activities in Stockholm, as no separate
Stockholm Federation exists. Among the various
activities are Israeli Independence Day celebrations,
a Hebrew-speaking Circle, Hebrew courses, a lecture
series and fund-raising campaigns. The Federation was
activated on behalf of Syrian and Russian Jewry and

42

was the initiator and organizer of various demonstrations and meetings. Contact with all the small communities is maintained by the Zionist Federation, and organizational as well as cultural assistance is provided, both through the Federation directly and through the Israeli ambassador and Jewish Agency shlichim. An important task of the Zionist Federation has been to assist in the integration of the Polish immigrants. Although paradoxical, in light of the anti-Israel ideology held by many post-1968 immigrants, it was the Jewish Agency shaliach who succeeded in forming the Polish student club in Stockholm, establishing ties between this group and other youth, and in serving as a catalyst for bringing Polish adults closer to the community, both through encouraging fresh attempts at contact by the Community and in opening up his house for cultural gatherings.[89]

The Zionist Federation works closely with the Israel fund-raising organizations (Keren Hayesod and Keren Kayemet LeIsrael), both of which are represented on the Federation board. WIZO raises money annually for its projects in Israel, and in addition there are campaigns for Youth Aliyah and ORT projects. Most of the responsibility for and work in carrying out the various fund-raising drives rests with the leadership of the Zionist Federation. Keren Kayemet LeIsrael has offices in Stockholm, Göteborg and Mälmo, and each of these cities runs its own campaign. [90]

WIZO

The first WIZO group in Sweden was founded in 1931. During the Nazi era, WIZO took an active part in various relief and assistance activities given to the incoming refugee groups, serving in rotation as "neighborly helpers," running a canteen in Stockholm, and organizing regular visits to Jewish women in neighboring refugee camps, acting as hostesses for refugee couples marrying in Sweden and supporting the medical rehabilitation program of tuberculosis patients, mainly children, in a Mälmo sanitarium.

Today WIZO has about 1,700 members and is the largest single Jewish organization in the country. Some of its leadership hold positions on the WIZO World Executive. The organization has a Jewish cultural and educational program for Swedish Jewish women, and also seems to serve as a unifying social force within the community. Branches of WIZO are active in Stockholm, Göteborg, and Mälmo, and smaller groups exist in Boras, Hälsingborg, Konkoping, Karlstad, Sundsvall, Uppsala, and Ubrige.[91] At a recent congress of Inter-Nordic WIZO, of which Swedish WIZO is a constituent, a major debate centered around the prospect of including non-Jews as members. Although the bill was finally defeated, the discussion itself pointed to the high degree of assimilation apparent both in WIZO's membership and in the community.[92]

The Jewish Press

Several Jewish periodicals appear in Sweden. The Judisk Kronika is an independently managed newspaper, in which the Zionist Federation pays for one page. At one time the paper came out about twenty times a year but now appears monthly. The Judisk Kronika is currently undergoing a serious economic crisis.[93]

The Community publishes a bulletin four to six times a year, called the Forsamlingsbladet. The Scandinavian B'nai Brith organ, B'nai Brith Nyt, published in Copenhagen, is distributed to members in Sweden. The Stockholm chapter of Bnei Akiva publishes a monthly newspaper. Until 1973, SJUF published a magazine; since then the Stockholm club includes one page on SJUF activities in its own newspaper, Synenegi, which is distributed throughout the country. The Jewish Center paper, called Centerbladet, is published six times a year and is sent throughout Scandinavia. Only since the wave of Polish Jewish immigration to Sweden have Yiddish language newspapers, printed in Paris, been sold freely at newsstands.[94]

Communal Finances

The local Communities rely mainly on the Community membership tax for their funds. The assessment base for such dues is income as reported to the income tax authorities, from which family and personal allowances are deducted. The government turns over income tax declarations of Community members to the Communities for Community tax assessment. Size of the dues varies from community to community, with the highest percentage paid in Mälmo. Membership dues in 1964 were as follows: 2.7 percent of gross income in Stockholm and a sliding tax with a top rate of 3.7 percent in Göteborg and 4.4 percent in Mälmo. By 1972, as a result of recession hitting the country, dues were reduced to 2.4 percent in Stockholm and reached something in excess of 4 percent in Mälmo.

Since 1948, the Swedish government has not allowed income tax deductions to charitable or religious institutions. Much discussion has been held about whether to permit non-members of the Communities (those who do not pay taxes) to benefit from communal services. The Mälmo dispute, referred to earlier, reached such proportions that leaders suggested obtaining police assistance in preventing non-Community members from praying in the synagogue. Other suggestions in most communities have included charging very high fees for services to non-Community members. Many Swedish Jews belong to the Communities solely or chiefly in order to receive Jewish burial rites. No matter how assimilated, most Jews wish to be buried Jewishly.

Another means of obtaining funds for Community and other local needs is through special drives for capital investment purposes. Usually pledges for large amounts are obtained in the form of annual subscriptions. Bazaars and other fund-raising devices are also employed.

Independent bodies are managed by special associations, such as the old age home, the nursing home, day school and kindergarten. They use the same methods as the Community and other organizations to finance their operating expenses. The Hillel School receives subventions from the government and the American Joint Distribution Committee; nevertheless, in order to meet expenses, it, like the kindergarten, charges very high fees. The Community helps meet the high cost of transportation to the school from the many districts of Stockholm to which Jews have migrated.

The work of fund-raising for Israel is done by volunteers who are organized and aided by an Israeli shaliach in Stockholm. The most important organization collecting for Israel needs is the Keren Hayesod-Magbit. The size of contributions varies according to the economic conditions in Sweden and the security and social situation in Israel.[95] After the Six Day War in 1967, the number of contributors rose by about 40 percent. Many contributors to Magbit are only partly Jewish or not Jewish at all. Other organizations collecting money for Israel include Keren Kayemet LeIsrael, WIZO, the Swedish Friends of the Hebrew University, Makkabi, ORT, plus several small organizations which solicit funds through the mail or through individuals, whether local or from Israel.[96] Following the Yom Kippur War in 1973, the Stockholm Community made a loan to Israel of SK 2 million and I.K. Makkabi raised SK 12,000. In 1975, Keren Kayemet LeIsrael in Sweden planted a forest in Israel, thanking the Swedish people "for their humanitarian efforts during the past thirty years."[97]

Many communal, educational, social, and youth projects are supported through the American Jewish Joint Distribution Committee, and until 1964, through tbe Claims Conference.

Governance of the Jewish Community

Due to the limited size of the Swedish Jewish Community and the fact that the majority of the Jewish population is located within the Stockholm area, that city has become the focal point of Jewish leadership in the country and leaders of the Stockholm Community have accepted leadership roles in a variety of Jewish activities simultaneously.

Three parties compete for control of the Stockholm Jewish Community (Mosaiska Forsamligen i Stockholm). Until the mid-1960's they were separated by social and ideological differences but more recently the lines of demarcation have blurred, as young native-born Swedish Jews have risen to leadership positions in all three.

The "Responsibility for the Future" or "Liberal Judaism" party was traditionally composed of old-time Jewish families of Western European origin who followed the Reform or Liberal approach to Judaism. Leaders of the Liberal Party often tended to perceive themselves as a social elite and accepted their leadership role as an act of noblesse oblige. More recently, however, the party has come to include a sizable number of East Europeans as well. Mr. Gunnar Josephson, head of the party for years, served as President of the Stockholm Jewish Community from 1936 in 1962, and again following the 1966 elections.

"Living Judaism" is a Zionist-inspired party which strives for intensification of traditional Jewish life and a Zionist-oriented philosphy. Originally, party members were East European post-1945 immigrants, but today there is a sizable number of West-Europeans as well. Generally, members of the Forenigen Chinuch, leaders of the Zionist Federation and members of the two Orthodox synagogues in the Community belong to "Living Judaism."

47

The "Rallying" or "Unity" Party is composed of younger families of all religious persuasions, native-born children of both East and West Europeans, who, in joining together in a separate party, represent a voice in communal politics which might go unheard were they to merge into the predominantly older groups. This party has gained strength since its inception in 1968.

The 1968 elections for the Stockholm Jewish Community brought a decisive turn in the communal leadership. "Responsibility for the Future" won ten seats, "Living Judaism" won nine, the "Rallying Party" won four and a splinter faction won two. The four parties formed two coalitions with "Living Judaism" and the "Rallying Party" combining to form a bloc of thirteen seats and the other two parties combining to form a bloc of twelve. A struggle ensued to determine whether the chairman of the Community would be chosen from the largest party or the largest coalition. The decision was important, for it would determine the degree of Jewishness of the community. The final choice was from the "Living Judaism"-"Rallying" coalition.[98] A similar communal leadership structure was produced in the wake of the 1974 elections.

In general, the leadership of Swedish Jewry tends to perpetuate itself and there is little rotation of offices. It appears, however, that activity in some groups serves as a springboard to others -- Forenigen Chinuch to "Living Judaism," membership on the Executive of SJUF (Scandinavian Youth Organization) to leadership in the Communities and Zionist Federation. The most active member of the Swedish Jewish community today has served as chairman of the Zionist Federation, the Community, and international communal bodies.

There are no formal divisions of power or functions between men and women, nevertheless, traditionally, women tend to hold social service positions, while men run the political and fund-raising organizations.

Great efforts have been made, especially in the past eight years, to develop a cadre of young leadership. Some Stockholm leaders feel that while the Community has succeeded in activating new leadership in their 40's and 50's, it will face a leadership crisis in the 1980's, when there will be no leadership to replace them.[99] Others feel that at least Stockholm and the other large communities as well, now have young professional Swedish-Jewish leadership, at least in terms of youth work and Jewish education and that the future leadership picture looks less bleak than in the past.[100] Everyone agrees, however, that the future of leadership of small communities is indeed grim since committed young people generally move to the larger communities or to Israel and are not being replaced. Those who remain take relatively little interest in Jewish affairs.[101]

Many of the frictions within the various factions composing the Jewish communities have been alluded to, such as the differing interpretations of Jewish identity and survival, as seen through the eyes of the pre-war and post-war populations, and the personal charges against the pre-war leadership in failing to save more Jews.

The Central Council of Swedish Jewish Communities represents the local Jewish Communities throughout the country, at least formally. The Zionist Federation of Sweden represents all communities. In addition to the main branch of <u>Keren Kayemet LeIsrael</u> in Stockholm, other branches are active in Malmö and Göteborg and separate drives are held in each of these communities. All WIZO groups are united under a national council; local chapters exist in Stockholm, Göteborg, Malmö, Boras, Hâlsingborg, Konköping, Karlstad, Kristianstad, Sundsval, and Uppsala. The <u>Keren Hayesod-Magbit</u> Board meets in Stockholm, but has members from other communities as well. Members of other communities are active on the Board of Deputies and various committees of the Stockholm Jewish Community.

Jewish Education

The Jewish Pedagogical and Resource Center is a joint project of the American Joint Distribution Committee, the Youth and Hechalutz Department and the local Jewish communities of Scandinavia. Its goals are to translate materials of use to Jewish youth and adult organizations in Judaism, Jewish History, Zionism, and Israel and to develop an audiovisual center for such material. The Center hopes to train youth leaders in the use of such material. Much discussion was held as to the correct location for such a center, especially in choosing between Stockholm and Mälmo. Finally Mälmo was chosen, for the following reasons: a) Stockholm, being the center of Scandinavian Jewry, may be "top heavy" as far as centralization goes; b) Mälmo, located in southern Sweden, is much more centrally located geographically for all of Scandinavia; c) Mälmo was very interested in hosting the center. The starting budget (1975) for the center is $150,000, divided between AJDC, the Jewish Agency and the local communities. The center's director is the youth worker at the Community Center and is able to use its facilities for the center.

The Pedagogic Center is part of the Jewish Programs Materials Project (JPMP), a world-wide endeavor sponsored by the AJDC and COJO (through the European Association of Jewish Community Centers), to coordinate the world-wide use of educational materials. The JPMP promotes European regional seminars for professional and semi-professional youth leaders. In 1973-1974, five regional seminars were held in which representatives from Denmark, Sweden, Norway and Finland participated. Israel JPMP seminars are also held for smaller European communities, specifically for professional directors and young key leaders. In the August, 1975, seminar there were participants from Stockholm, Lund, Malmö and Göteborg.

Swedish Jewry participates in World ORT and the World Jewish Congress. The Swedish branch of WJC is not a membership organization but is activated upon necessity. It is actually a one-man enterprise.[102] When WJC held its convention in Stockholm in 1959 it received the unprecedented honor of being permitted to hold its meetings in the Swedish Parliament.

The Stockholm Community represents Sweden in the European Council of Jewish Community Services. The European Council, a deliberative forum for community leaders from some eighteen countries, is the successor to the Standing Conference of European Jewish Communities, organized by the American Joint Distribution Committee in the 1950's. In 1972, the European Council adopted a five year program providing for commissions on fund-raising, young leadership training and social services, as well as activating a Europe-Wide Jewish Community Centers Association.[103] Mr. Fritz Hollender, the outstanding leader of the Swedish community, has been a constant member of the European Council and in 1975, was serving as its chairman. In recent years the European Council for Jewish Community Services has jointly sponsored youth and educational projects such as the Scholar in Residence Project, in which Israeli intellectuals and artists spend three or four weeks in Scandinavian Jewish communities.

COJO (The World Conference of Jewish Organizations) has recently joined the American Joint Distribution Committee, the Jewish Agency Youth and Hechalutz Department and local communities throughout Sweden in financing some of the activities for youth.

The American Joint Distribution Committee has been extremely active in helping create organized Jewish life in Sweden. In the years up to 1964, the Claims Conference and the Joint Distribution Committee supplied approximately 20 percent of the Swedish Jewish community's total consolidated income. While

51

the community has since become self-supporting, the Joint Distribution Committee has remained active in providing funds for educational and youth work. Following the wave of Polish Jewish immigration, it has concentrated on activities serving to advance the integration of Polish youth into the community, as well as furthering general Jewish youth work. In 1970, together with the Jewish Agency and the local Jewish communities, the Joint Distribution Committee established the Schwartz Program at the Paul S. Baerwold School of Social Work of the Hebrew University to train community leaders from Great Britian and Scandinavia.

In addition to JDC's support of the Pedagogic and Resource Center and the Jewish Programs Materials Project, it has also assisted in the purchase of a youth clubhouse in Uppsala and the support of a part-time youth leader there. It also assists in the support of the Hillel Day School.[104]

HIAS used to be very active in Sweden, in connection with the Stockholm Community Emigration Bureau, which was finally closed down in 1964.

As a consequence of the assassination of the Swedish diplomat Count Folke Bernadotte in Jerusalem in 1948, the Swedish government was slow to recognize the newly established State of Israel (de jure recognition was extended in July, 1950). The general attitude of the Swedish people to the Jewish State has always been friendly, characteristic of its liberal philosophy and labor-oriented government. Trade between the two countries abounds and Swedish tourists find Israel a popular attraction.

The Jewish community's involvement in the reality of Israel is reflected in its own struggle between Jewish identification and assimilation. Beginning with interest in Zionism after World War II, paralleling a resurgence of activity in Jewish life and community organization, and climaxing with stronger commitment both to Israel and Judaism following the Six Day War, the Swedish Jewish community has established a number of Israel-oriented organizations and fund-raising campaigns, to which contributions have steadily grown both in number of contributors and amount contributed. Whereas in the early days of Israel's existence few Swedish Jews considered aliyah, today it has become at least a serious consideration in the minds of many Jewishly-committed Swedish youth and young adults.

Summary

A small minority community placed in the midst of an essentially liberal and assimilating host society, Swedish Jewry has always been beset by the problems of identification and group survival. Overcoming the enormous difficulties and responsibilities placed on it as a center for the ingathering of the victims of the Holocaust, the Swedish community has not only retained its identity but, especially since 1967, has made great strides in intensifying the character of its Jewish communal life and attempting to provide the basis among its youth for future communal participation. If, before World War II, the community tended to be isolationist, since then it has taken an increasingly important role in rallying behind the Jewish cause, whether locally, in Israel, or among the persecuted elements of World Jewry.

However, many factors hamper the development of a truly integrated and vital community. Among these are the high rate of intermarriage and assimilation, the distribution of half the country's Jewish population in areas where there may be little or no contact with other Jews, the increasing numbers of aliyah among committed youth, and the strains and conflicts within the community's leadership. Although predictions for the future are difficult to make, the Swedish Jewish community, if aided by leadership from abroad and revitalized by integration of its new immigrant population, might prove able to overcome its difficulties of numbers and remain a vital community in coming generations.

THE JEWISH COMMUNITY OF DENMARK

Adina Weiss Liberles

From its inception, the Jewish community of Denmark has enjoyed comparative religious and ethnic freedom within a friendly and sympathetic host culture. Unlike the circumstances in most areas of Jewish settlement, Denmark's Jews never feared physical annihilation or even virulent anti-Semitism at the hands of their own countrymen. And when the threat of destruction appeared from foreign sources, Danish Jewry experienced a sense of concern and brotherhood from its neighbors that has become legendary.

In such an atmosphere of acceptance, it is no wonder that a large segment of the Jewish community has continually converted to Christianity and completely assimilated into the general culture. What is, perhaps, more amazing is the fact that the community has survived, as a result of a sometimes small but committed number of native-born Jews, augmented by new waves of immigration at times of internal crises of survival bringing fresh blood and renewed commitment to organized Jewish life.

The Development of the Community

Oldest of the Scandinavian communities, the first Jews settled in Denmark in 1622, when Christian IV invited a group of wealthy Portuguese Jews from Amsterdam and Hamburg to settle in the town of Glückstadt, in Holstein, in exchange for their capital with which to finance the king's war. By 1657, under the reign of Frederik III, Sephardic Jews were assured of a reasonable security throughout the land and were able to establish a recognizable Jewish community,[1] but poorer Ashkenazic Jews who had entered the country illegally were expelled.

On March 29, 1814, the Danish Parliament passed a Law of Freedom, granting religious freedom to all inhabitants. The community, which until then had been an officially recognized autonomous structure, lost its autonomy; thenceforth determined by royal ordinance. The office of Chief Rabbi was inaugurated. The Constitution of Denmark, signed on June 5, 1849, granted Jews full citizenship with all its political and religious rights and privileges.[2]

The Danish attitude toward and protection of its Jews in the face of Nazi persecution has become legendary. While the Germans began systematically trampling down the rights of Jews in Germany, King Christian X took part in a festive service marking the hundredth anniversary of the Great Synagogue in Copenhagen. The Danish authorities made efforts to suppress any anti-Semitic tendencies that filtered into the country. Some refugees from German persecution were admitted to the country.

When Denmark was occupied by the Germans in 1940, the Jewish population numbered approximately 8,000 persons, or a little under two per thousand of the total Danish population. For more than three years the Germans treated Denmark as a showplace protectorate, claiming that the Danes were true

59

Aryans, but probably more likely in order to exploit more fully the rich agricultural resources and considerable shipbuilding facilities the country offered. The Danes insisted on full protection of the rights of Jewish citizens. But by 1943, the Danish underground had become open in its hostility to the Nazis and much harsher political and economic restrictions were placed on the country, including the Jews. On September 28, 1943, the German in charge of recruiting Danish merchant shipping for the Occupation, George Ferdinand Duckwitz, secretly informed the Danish government that mass deportations of Danish Jews to concentration camps were to begin immediately. When Jews assembled in the synagogue the next day for High Holiday services, they were warned of the impending danger. A mass rescue operation, led by the Danish underground, placed almost the entire Jewish population in hiding with Danish families along the coast of the Oeresund Strait, separating Denmark from Sweden, and within a period of three weeks ferried them to nearby neutral Sweden. Only 470 Jews were rounded up by the Gestapo in Denmark and sent to Theresienstadt Camp in Czechoslovakia, where the vast majority managed to survive the war.[3] When the Jews returned to Denmark in May, 1945, they received a warm reception from the Danes who had safeguarded and tended their property for them during their absence. Christian clergy had gathered together Torah scrolls and their ornaments and hidden them in a Copenhagen church for safekeeping during the war.

Only incomplete statistics are available on the number of Jews living in Denmark today for the following reasons: The last time a question about religious affiliation appeared in the Danish population census was 1921; intermarriage has been so prevalent that at least 200,000 Danes can trace some Jewish blood in their ancestry but do not consider themselves Jewish,[4] while, on the other hand, Jewish partners of mixed marriages are still considered part of the community, sometimes bringing up their children as Jews; questions have often been raised as to whether many of the Polish immigrants who arrived after 1968 are really Jewish; except for membership in the Jewish community of Copenhagen and registration of children within its ranks at birth, there is no accurate way of determining the size of the current Jewish population.

The contemporary Danish Jewish community is comprised of four different waves of immigration. The first consists of Portuguese, Dutch and German Jews entering the country in the eighteenth century. At that time the Copenhagen Jewish community grew from eleven households to 270, with an additional sixty-two in the provinces; this number represented a total of about 1,830 persons. In 1834 the Jewish population had grown to 4,072.[5] By the twentieth century there was a decrease in Jewish population; in 1901 it was only 3,476.[6] Undoubtedly the decrease is attributed to the vast number of intermarriages and high rate of assimilation that took place in the nineteenth century, as a result of full civil equality granted in 1814 and its resultant social integration.

The second stratum of the contemporary Jewish community is composed of East European Jews who entered Denmark between 1901 and 1921, and their children. An estimated 3,146 Jews crossed the borders into Denmark, 2,615 of whom were refugees fleeing Russian pogroms, and 531 who were World War I refugees. The Russian immigration increased the Jewish population to a total of approximately 6,000 Jews, or 1.8 per thousand of the general population (as compared with 1.4 per thousand in 1901).[7]

The third stratum of the Jewish community reached Denmark as a consequence of World War II. Following Hitler's rise to power, approximately 4,500 Jews entered Denmark from Germany, Austria and Czechoslovakia in the period preceding Denmark's occupation. Of this number, about 3,000 continued their journey to other countries, leaving only about 1,500 Jewish refugees, or less than five percent of the foreigners in Denmark.[8] Under the agricultural training program established by the Zionist movement under the auspices of the Committee for the 4th of May, 1933, approximately 1,500 young Jews entered

61

Denmark for a year.[9] Slightly over three hundred children found refuge in Denmark through a scheme coordinated by Youth Aliyah, the Women's League for Peace and Freedom, and the Jewish Women's Association.

Swedish refugee files compiled after Danish Jewry's escape to Sweden in 1943 register 7,220 Danish Jews and 686 non-Jewish Danes connected with them by family ties. The Danish government registered 475 Jews deported to Theresienstadt. Another three hundred Jews left Denmark during the occupation, died on the way to Sweden or Theresienstadt, or remained in Denmark.[10]

At the close of the war, the entire Danish refugee population in Sweden, those who had successfully escaped Denmark in 1943, and the Theresienstadt survivors who had been brought to Sweden a few months before the war ended, returned to Denmark, accompanied by less than one thousand other Jewish refugees. From then until 1968, few Jews immigrated to Denmark, except for fifty Hungarian Jews fleeing the Hungarian Revolution in 1956 and small numbers of Israelis.

Thus, at the end of 1968, the Danish Jewish population numbered between 6,000 and 7,000 persons, 25 percent descendants of the early Danish Jewish families, 67 percent East European emigrants and descendants, and 8 percent World War II refugees.[11] Figures for membership of the Copenhagen Jewish Community for 1976 showed seven thousand members.

The last stratum of Danish Jewish population today is that of Polish Jews who immigrated to Denmark following the Polish government's persecution of Polish Jewry in 1968. An estimated 2,500 Jews entered the country in the next three years.

Since 1948, about six hundred Danish Jews have emigrated to Israel, most of them in the early 1950's or in the years following the Six Day War.

In 1693, a Jewish community was organized in the city of Fredericiah, in Juttland. The subsequent early Danish Jewish community was scattered throughout the country, in as many as sixty provincial towns and villages, with settlement in Copenhagen only after 1787. But whereas in 1834, 40 percent (1,607 of the country's Jews) lived outside Copenhagen, only 7.1 percent (245 persons) did so in 1901).[12] This internal migrational shift occurred near the end of the nineteenth century, reflecting the development of the Danish economy and the growing concentration of businesses in Copenhagen.

Today about 1 percent of the Jewish population resides outside the capital, with by far the greatest number of those centered in Århus, Denmark's second largest city, which has become an important absorption center for the Polish Jewish immigrants. Although there are Jews living in other towns as well, except for Århus, no full-time Jewish activities are conducted outside of Copenhagen. The town of Hornbaek has become a popular Jewish holiday resort area where many Jewish religious, cultural, educational and social activities take place during the summer months.

In Copenhagen itself, the Jewish quarter in the old part of the city had begun to dissolve as early as 1930,[13] and when the Jews returned in 1945, they continued to populate all neighborhoods. Today there is no such thing as a Jewish section within the city itself, and although one may find many Jews living in particular suburbs, they do not form Jewish neighborhoods. Almost all Jewish communal services are centralized, sometimes presenting problems of easy accessibility.

The number of Jewish births in Denmark is between sixty and seventy a year. For several years it seemed that such a small birth rate could not sustain the size of the community. However it now seems to be rising slightly.[14]

The first Jewish immigrants were admitted to Denmark because of their wealth and international connections. Soon merchants and craftsmen followed, introducing into Denmark new industries, such as tobacco, textiles, and agricultural implements, as well as establishing trading houses and financial enterprises.[15]

At the end of the eighteenth century the Jewish community mirrored the Danish agrarian reforms and economic prosperity which contributed to the rising standard of living. In the ensuing period of social and political crises in the early part of the nineteenth century, the Jews continued to prosper. This was the case again in the second half of the century when Denmark was defeated in the war with Prussia and Austria, destroying the economic structure which had been based on fishing and agricultural exports to Europe. But other areas of agricultural production increased and were exported to England. The Jews, active in this change, helped save the economy, as well as continuing to develop the nation's financial resources.[16] The Russian Jewish wave of immigration brought a return to crafts and a development of the garment trade.

Today, the Jews of Denmark, like those in other Scandinavian countries, enjoy stable economic prosperity, although there are proportionately fewer wealthy Jews in Denmark than in Norway. The majority of Jewish breadwinners today are businessmen, a large minority enter the free professions. The number in the latter category is much larger than a generation ago. Most Danes leave school after ten grades, whereupon they attend technical or trade schools or enter the job market; the Jews have a larger percentage of students graduating from college preparatory schools.

Intermarriage and Assimilation

Once Jews were awarded their civil rights in Denmark at the beginning of the nineteenth century, they began to assimilate. The economic prosperity

64

felt by Danish Jews in the second half of the century was accompanied by a rise in their cultural and social level. Several hundred of the more affluent Jewish families began to embrace Christianity, although they gained little material advantage from so doing. Intermarriage became increasingly prevalent, so that by 1880 an estimated thirty percent of Jews marrying had non-Jewish partners. By 1921 the estimated figure had reached more than fifty percent of the old Danish families.[17] Indeed, figures for the Jewish population in the late 1960's show that only one-fourth of the community was of West European descent.

For several years after their immigration to Denmark the Jews kept within the Jewish fold. By now, however, little distinction is made between West and East European Jews with regard to assimilation and intermarriage. No accurate figures on the rate of intermarriage have been published, but it is estimated that between thirty and 75 percent of Danish Jews intermarry.[18] If a Jewish woman marries a non-Jew, their children are counted within the ranks of the Jewish community; if the non-Jewish partner in a marriage converts, the community does not consider the marriage to have been a "mixed marriage." Converted spouses are readily accepted into the community. However, most non-Jewish partners do not convert and although the Jewish partner may remain a member of the community, the family rarely affiliates with it. Many Israelis have settled in Denmark, often marrying non-Jews, some of whom convert to Judaism (in 1975 five of the eleven conversions performed in the community were in this category).

Despite the small percentage of Jews within the general population of approximately five million Danes, the Jewish presence is felt within Danish society. In the past decade there have been a substantial number of Jews in high civil service positions (e.g. government ministers, state comptroller, Members of Parliament). Several Jewish professors have become famous in their fields, especially in jurisprudence, and some Jews have become leaders in commerce, particularly in the fur trade.[19]

65

Everyone born of a Jewish mother or converted to Judaism according to halacha (Jewish religious law) is considered a Jew by the community. Jewish marriages performed by the rabbis are recognized as binding by the state and no civil ceremony is required.

All Danish Jews, especially the older settlers, have an extremely patriotic national identification, considering themselves Danes of the Jewish religious faith. In fact, their Jewishness is often expressed more as an accident of birth, not to be denied or to be ashamed of, but as an interesting curiosity rather than the result of a religious commitment or a strong expression of peoplehood with Jews throughout the world.[20] Due to the lack of historical or contemporary anti-Semitism in the country, because of the powerful support the Jews received as a respected and wanted element of Danish society in the face of Nazi oppression, and as a consequence of the general non-religious and open society of Denmark, the negative pressures of the host society which so often motivate a need or desire for Jewish unity do not exist in Denmark. It is necessary to understand this acceptance of themselves as Danes to understand their relations both with each other and with world Jewry.

Every Jew wishing to opt out of membership in the Jewish community is required by Danish law to write a formal letter of resignation to the Chief Rabbi who often discusses such a move with the applicant. If the applicant persists in his wish, the rabbi then submits his report to the Board of Delegates and the resignation is recorded in the community protocols. The actual numbers of those opting out is quite small, about forty a year, and many who do so rejoin later on. In order to benefit from any communal services, such as synagogue, school, many organizations, burial benefits, etc., one must belong to the community. As assimilated as many Danish Jews are, most still wish to have a Jewish burial. (It is possible to get a cemetery plot as a non-member, but the fee is prohibitive.)

Anti-Semitism and Jewish-Danish Relations

In the first period of Jewish settlement in Denmark, Jews faced economic, social and civil restrictions, as they did elsewhere. Yet, their position was better than in many other countries; Jews were never forced to live in ghettos, their internal affairs were unsupervised until emancipation and they were granted a degree of autonomy in matters of administration.[21] In the second half of the eighteenth century Jews began studying at the University of Copenhagen, and by the end of that century had begun to attend Danish elementary and secondary schools. The Danish artisans' cooperatives were opened to Jews at this time.

Although in 1814 rights had been assured, in the early nineteenth century there was a rise in anti-Semitic feeling, expressed by a "literacy war" in 1813 and a form of pogrom against Jewish businesses following the 1918 "Hepp-Hepp" riots in Germany,[22] repeated again in 1831 during widespread economic difficulties. Although Danish Jewry itself supported the new Reform movement in religion, some practices, such as the ceremony of confirmation, were forced upon it by the Danish authorities. Politically, while it is true that ever since 1814 the Jews enjoyed political rights, nonetheless, several decades passed until they achieved full political equality. As the economic and cultural level of the Jewish community continued to improve in the second half of the nineteenth century, so did their absorption into the host community, with little increase of anti-Semitism, although emerging movements in Germany at the end of the century did have some repercussions in Denmark. On the contrary, at the end of the nineteenth century and the beginning of the twentieth, the Chief Rabbis of Denmark actively sought the aid of the Danish Royal Family in interceding with the Russian government on behalf of Russian Jewry.

Anti-Jewish feeling in the first quarter of the twentieth century was more actively expressed by the old-time Danish families against the newcomers than by the Danish Christians. But by the eve of the Second World War relationships between the different segments of the Jewish community had improved. As German anti-Semitism spread its propaganda to other nations, an ideological debate arose within the Danish Jewish community as to the most effective means of combatting anti-Semitism within Denmark. The newer wave of Danish Jewry, together with many old families, fought to publicize the threat and militantly oppose it. Many members of the community, including most of the elected leaders, believed in "quiet diplomacy," which was interpreted by the more militant element as an attempt to ignore the situation.

In 1936 a new Danish edition of The Protocols of the Elders of Zion was published; this was followed by a strong public declaration by several leading clergymen against this and other anti-Semitic literature. An amendment to the Criminal Law of 1939 subjected to fine or imprisonment anyone who by virtue of false rumors or slander incited hatred against any section of the Danish population by reason of its religion, origin, or citizenship.[23]

However, the Danish authorities in the period before occupation laid down severe criteria for accepting Jewish refugees, granting permits only to relatives of Danish citizens resident in the country and whose economic support could be guaranteed in advance.[24] One must, however, see these restrictions in light of the widespread unemployment and serious economic problems besetting the country at the time.

In 1952 the Danish Nazi Party was revived, but it was met with little enthusiasm. The following year it began publishing a pamphlet, Fadrelandet. The magazine is read by only about forty people.[25] A memorial meeting was held by the Party in 1960 for the fifteenth anniversary of Hitler's death. Neo-Nazi leaders are periodically jailed for publishing anti-Semitic statements.[26] Other than these sporadic occurrances, there has been no increase in anti-Semitism in recent years.

As a community the Jews do not affilate with any one political party or group, although many support the leading Social Democratic Party, which has always been vocally pro-Israel. Numerically the Jews are too small a group to constitute a "Jewish vote" even if they so desired, but, in any case, such an act would run strongly counter to their feeling of being Danes. Furthermore, their educational and professional backgrounds are very similar to those of non-Jewish Danes. All these socio-economic factors that often generate anti-Semitic feelings in communities where the Jews can be classified as "different" in some way from the general population are generally absent in Denmark.

At present, non-Jews do not generally concern themselves with Jewish life. However they strongly supported Israel in the Six Day and Yom Kippur wars and actively demonstrated against Soviet oppression of its Jews, as well as opening its gates to any Polish Jewish refugees wishing to enter in 1968, and subsequent years. Locally, large conflicts within the Jewish community are reported in the newspapers as general interest information. The community is conscious of its Jewishness and sensitive to public references to its special community character and affairs, feeling that such publicity might at some future point, provide the basis for anti-Jewish feeling of some kind or lead to a sense of ridicule and loss of respect for the Jews. We shall see how this has affected community relations.

The Polish Immigration

In 1966, the Polish government began another of its extended anti-Semitic campaigns, this time leveled at Jewish members of the Communist Party or well-established figures in Polish intellectual life. Following the Six Day War, when the Polish anti-Zionist campaign intensified, Jews were permitted to leave the country if they renounced Polish

69

citizenship, abandoned their possessions and declared themselves Zionist, having a wish to settle in Israel.

Most of the Jews leaving Poland in 1968-1971 were middle-aged, loyal Communists and steadfast Poles, who had heretofore renounced their Judaism in favor of Polish Communism. Many were married to non-Jewish Poles or were children of such marriages.[27] Israel was rejected by many of them because they were not Zionists, they did not feel Jewish, they feared discrimination against the non-Jewish members of their families, and because they wished to remain in cosmopolitan Europe.

Why have close to 2,500 Jews settled in Denmark, and thousands more in the other Scandinavian countries? Sweden, Norway, and especially Denmark were among the few nations to welcome them. The United States would not accept members of the Communist Party. On the other hand Denmark had been a symbol of tolerance toward Jews dating from World War II, had opened its doors to the Poles with no restrictions; the standard of living was high and the government provided excellent conditions for refugee assimilation.

Indeed, the Danish government provided a daily financial stipend, free public transportation, and free tuition for language study. The Danish social welfare system is immediately available to refugees. Furthermore, the Poles received medical aid, school and university grants, and for the elderly, state pensions after one year's residence. Benefits are provided under law until the refugees find employment.

The Danish government spent about $4,000,000 annually between 1968 and 1970 to assist the Polish refugees, the money being administered by the Refugee Council, a private coordinating body of eleven voluntary organizations, including the Danish Red Cross and the Jewish community. In conjunction with international Jewish refugee organizations, the Council arranged payments to the Polish government for exit visas and paid travel costs. In Denmark it arranged for the reception, temporary housing, language instruction and various financial and social benefits, including providing for excursions, social affairs, weddings and study abroad.[28]

The American Joint Distribution Committee, together with the Jewish Agency, have played a large role in providing financial resources and professional staff to work with the new immigrants, but demanding that the local Jewish community also accept its financial responsibility in integrating the newcomers.[29]

Response from the Danish Jews has been mixed. Some blame the new immigrants for having abandoned their Judaism in the past; some feel that the Poles must first demonstrate their willingness to become practicing Jews before being considered worthy of aid. But others realize the energy a new wave of immigration could contribute to the community if channeled properly. The official community response has been to accept Polish immigrants into the communal school and community organizations, but not to actively woo their participation. Soon after the immigrants first arrived, daily kosher meals at a nominal cost were provided at the Jewish Community Center, but attendance gradually tapered off. Several attempts were made to provide cultural and social activities for the newcomers, such as "Contact," a series of lectures and social programs held at the Jewish Community Center. The Polish Jewish Social Club was inaugurated in an effort to bring Danish and Polish Jews together, but few Danish Jews showed a desire to attend.[30]

It seems that within the last two years, the Polish immigrants are slowly accepting and being accepted into the community. In 1974 the Joint and the Jewish Agency appointed a shaliach to Denmark whose work would be divided between general community functions and special work with the Polish Jews. Immigrant youth have become the activists of the Jewish Student Club. In 1975, four of the seven Danish participants in the Youth and Pioneering

71

sponsored Leadership Training Seminar in Israel were of Polish origin. Greater understanding and cooperation are now apparent between the Danish Jewish community and the Federation of Polish Jews in Denmark. As of 1976 close to five hundred immigrants had formally joined the community and a provision is now being passed permitting the immigrants full membership at a community tax rate of half the normal amount.[31] About sixty Polish children study in the Jewish Day School, many on scholarship. Hopes for even greater integration have been voiced since the election of a Polish Jew to the 1975 Board of Delegates from the Youth List.

Chief Rabbi Bent Melchior works closely with the Polish immigrants, and has been responsible for many of them obtaining government permission to reside in Copenhagen, the only real center of Jewish life.[32]

A new quasi-community has been established in Århus by its Polish Jewish inhabitants. The Federation of Polish Jews in Denmark has a community center there, where a number of monthly activities take place. On the High Holidays the Chief Rabbi assists the community in holding religious services and on Passover helps arrange for matzot to be brought in. Although Danish Jews also live in Århus, they do not participate in Jewish activities.

The Structure of the Danish Jewish Community

The Mosaic Community

The main institution of the Danish Jewish community is the Mosaic Community, to which all Danish Jews belong who have not officially opted out of membership. Its headquarters are in Copenhagen, but one may be a member and live elsewhere. At birth children are registered as community members and receive all the rights and privileges thereof except the ballot, which is theirs when they reach Danish voting age (twenty-one), if they have paid their communal dues.

The community is governed by a twenty-member Board of Delegates (Delegeret Forsamlingen), elected every two years. The Board of Delegates, in turn, elects a seven member Board of Representatives (Raprasentater Forsamlingen). The other ruling boards of the community are the seven-member Board of Gabayim of the Synagogue, jointly appointed by the Board of Representatives, the Board of Delegates and seat-holding male members of the synagogue; the five member Education Committee, appointed by the Board of Representatives, the Ministry of Education and the Board of Delegates; and the five-member Tax Committee, appointed by the Board of Representatives, the municipality and the Board of Delegates.

The Board of Delegates meets six to twelve times a year. It serves mainly as an advisory group to the Board of Representatives; in addition it approves the annual budget and any religious appointments.

The Board of Representatives governs the daily affairs of the community. Representatives head committees dealing with the Old Age Home, religious affairs, Jewish education, and cemeteries. It sets

73

Table 1. The Associational Structure of the
          Copenhagen Jewish Community[1]

The Electorate: Members in good standing of the Community who are 21 years of age or over

COMMUNITY BOARD OF DELEGATES	SYNAGOGUE BOARD OF GABAYIM

20 members
Chairman of the Board=
Chairman of the
Community
	7 members
	1 Rep. of the Board of
	   Representatives
	2 Reps. of the Board of
	   Delegates
	4 Reps. chosen by the
	   male seat-holding
	   members of the
	   synagogue

BOARD OF REPRESENTATIVES 7 members + Chairman of the Community

TAX COMMITTEE	EDUCATION COMMITTEE

5 members
1 Rep. of the Board of
   Representatives
4 Reps. approved by
   the Municipality
   of whom 2 are
   chosen by the
   Board of Delegates
	4 members
	1 Rep. of the Board of
	   Representatives
	2 Reps. chosen by the
	   the Ministry of
	   Education
	1 Rep. chosen by the
	   Board of Delegates

[1]From "The Jewish Community of Denmark," an unpublished
seminar paper submitted by Dov Levittan to Bar-Ilan
University, 1976.

74

the annual communal tax rate and works out the budget. In addition, the Board of Representatives represents the Danish Jewish community in dealings with the Danish government (through the Ministry of Religion), with the State of Israel (through the Israeli Embassy and through direct negotiations), and with other Jewish communities (through pan-Scandinavian councils and committees, ties with European and other international Jewish bodies, such as the American Joint Distribution Committee and the World Council of Synagogues). The Board of Representatives meets about three times a month.

Religious Affairs

As prescribed by the Law of Freedom (1814) and the Danish Constitution (1849), the Chief Rabbi of Copenhagen is the Chief Rabbi of Denmark and is responsible to the King as representative of Danish Jewry. He keeps the community records, called Ministerial Protocols, in which are registered all births, marriages, divorces and deaths in the Jewish community. When a child is born to members of the community, the rabbi forwards a copy of the birth certificate to the government, but the parents receive the official birth certificate directly from the office of the Jewish community. The Chief Rabbi has complete authority under law in his synagogue. He, plus two other scholars constitute a Bet Din for purposes of conversions and divorces. The Bet Din has almost never been used to settle civil disputes.

At present there is only one rabbi in the community, but a second (also Danish) is presently being trained in Israel under community sponsorship and will return to Denmark in the summer of 1976. The new Assistant Rabbi will work mostly in the fields of education and youth work. The previous Assistant Rabbi, an American, was dismissed a few years ago when he caused controversy in the community by riding the Copenhagen subways on Shabbat. (According to a minority Orthodox rabbinic position, using public

75

transportation is acceptable under certain provisions.) Such protestation is typical of the ambivalence under which the Danish Jewish community lives, since the vast majority of Danish Jews drive on the Sabbath themselves and never question the halachic objections to their actions.

The community synagogue, the Krystalgade Synagogue, was erected in 1833. The synagogue is governed by a seven member Board of Gabayim, chosen every four years by male synagogue members, the Board of Delegates and the Board of Representatives. One of the members of the Board of Gabayim sits on the Board of Representatives (with the title of Representative for Religious Affairs). All Gabayim are Sabbath observers. A movement is now under way to permit women to be synagogue members with full voting privileges.

The main synagogue serves as a "place of gathering" in the real sense of the term. If any unusual event occurs in the Jewish world, it is the first place to which the Jews turn, and as such, has come to represent the focal point for expression for solidarity with Israel and world Jewry. Most of the Jewish weddings in Denmark are performed in the synagogue. During the High Holy days the synagogue is filled to overflowing. Average attendance on regular Sabbaths is about three hundred -- a large percentage of the congregation. Young people, a substantial part of the worshippers, often lead the services.

Like all other Jewish communal institutions in Denmark, the synagogue is nominally Orthodox. It follows the Orthodox Altona-Hamburg ritual, has separate seating, a male choir, and uses no organ. As in all Danish houses of worship, the synagogue service includes a prayer for the welfare of the King; in addition, a prayer for Israel is recited. The weekly sermon is delivered in Danish. The majority of congregants are not Orthodox.

Not all members of the community are members of the main synagogue, although all main synagogue members must belong to the community. Members pay synagogue dues and potential members must often wait until a seat becomes vacant.

Historically, the Danish Jewish community struggled with its religious self image for some time. Until the end of the eighteenth century most Jews were Orthodox. But then German Reform became increasingly popular in Denmark, led by Mendel Levin Nathanson. Differences between the Reform and Orthodox elements became so irreconcilable that it took several years until a compromise could be reached, under Chief Rabbi Abraham Alexander Wolff,[33] who served the community for sixty-two years following his appointment in 1828. His first act, which united the community in common action was the building of a central synagogue to replace the one which had been destroyed by fire in 1790. (In the intervening years prayers had been conducted in fifteen different places.)

As a result of a different religious struggle in 1910, a second congregation was established in Copenhagen. This is a right-wing Orthodox group, called Machsike Hadas. The congregation has ties with the Agudat Yisrael and Lubovicher movements. Nearly all members of Machsike Hadas belong to the community, paying full taxes; in addition, they support their own institutions and functionaries. About one hundred families belong to this community.

Almost all Jewish boys in Denmark undergo the bar mitzvah ceremony and many girls are confirmed. Both ceremonies were at one time obligatory under Danish law, which required that all children receive a religious education of some kind as a prerequisite to applying for a marriage license. The Chief Rabbi gives a weekly three month course for pre-bar mitzvah boys and confirmands.[34]

There are two kosher butcher shops in Copenhagen, one under the supervision of the main community and the other supervised by the Machsike Hadas. In 1954, the Danish authorities wanted to replace traditional kosher slaughtering with the process of stunning

animals. Halachic slaughtering was finally permitted to continue if casting pens were used. The
London Board of Shechita furnished the Danish community with two such pens.[35]

According to the Constitution of the community,
any Jew in the community has the right to have a
memorial service held for him. There are two burial
societies in the Copenhaven community, one following
strictly Orthodox burial procedure and the other,
liberal. Members of the boards of the burial
societies are elected annually by the membership of
the societies, and following European tradition,
leaders deem it a privilege to serve on these boards.
The burial society boards are completely voluntary
groups.

Conversion to Judaism seems to have become a
popular consideration in the eyes of many Danes since
the end of World War II and the establishment of the
State of Israel. This is especially true of
non-Jewish youth who have spent time living and
working on Israeli kibbutzim. Conversions are conducted according to halacha and converts must promise to
keep the laws of kashrut and join the community.

Jewish Education

Jewish education in Denmark functioned in an
organized fashion by the end of the eighteenth
century. Until World War II Copenhagen had two Jewish
Day Schools, one for each sex. After the war, the
schools merged into one coeducational institution,
called the Caroline Skoline, covering the first seven
years of schooling. Although originally founded to
serve the community's poorer members, and to
"Danishize" the East Europeans, its high academic
rating serves to draw students to it, thus enabling
them to acquire deeper roots in Judaism.

78

Today, more than half the Jewish children in Copenhagen between the ages of five and fourteen attend the school. About ten years ago, perhaps as a result of the low birthrate, the school witnessed a decline in enrollment. Then there began a reverse trend, increasing interest was shown in Jewish education and enrollment increased from about one hundred pupils to nearly three hundred today. The school moved into its facilities in Spring 1974, with the building constructed to allow for the "open classroom" technique of education through grade 6. Class size is kept small, with parallel classes held in most grades. In 1975, the study program was extended to the end of grade 10.

The school follows the standard Danish curriculum for secular studies, often acting as innovator for the rest of the country. Its secular studies are financed by the Ministry of Education (approximately 85 percent of the budget). The Jewish community contributes about DK 30,000 annually and the remainder of expenses is met through tuition fees.

Governance of the school comes from the School Board, some of whose members are appointed by the Boards of Deputies and Representatives, while others are chosen directly by the parents.

Pupils study Jewish subjects between four and six hours a week depending on the age of the children. Studies include both Hebrew language and religious instruction, with efforts made to synthesize studies wherever possible. Boys are expected to wear skullcaps for Jewish studies and while eating, but the majority of pupils do not come from observant homes. With the program of studies increased to tenth grade, the school included in its curriculum in 1974-1975 a three week study period in Israel for the ninth grade class.

The headmaster of the school is not Jewish, but keeps a kosher home and is extremely knowledgeable about and close to Jewish life. About half the total staff of the school (Both Judaica and secular departments) are non-Jewish, but all Judaica teachers, about six or seven in number, must be observant Jews. Some are yeshiva graduates and most are graduates of Bnei Akiva. In the past, Israeli shlichim served as teachers, but by and large proved to be unsatisfactory, and now efforts are made to use local teachers. The teaching staff is very young; of the entire staff, only one has taught at the school over ten years. The community has made no effort to send teachers to Israel to train.

Jewish studies have not reached a very high level; therefore seldom becoming a motivating force in the students' lives. However, there has been notable improvement in the last few years. Raising the student age may allow for more in-depth education and commitment, as may the Israel study experience. On the other hand, older students may find themselves in a situation where, looking for ways to rebel as teenagers, school affiliation may turn their rebellion against the establishment concepts of religion and community. Whatever danger this may lead to, compensations will be made by giving Jewish teenagers easy access to other Jewish youth.[36]

There are three Jewish kindergartens in Copenhagen: the Caroline School runs a kindergarten for about forty children. Yeshurun Kindergarten is sponsored by Machsike Hadas, but also has a few children whose parents do not belong. A third, independent Jewish kindergarten operates in the suburb of Virum.

Machsike Hadas parents overwhelmingly send their children to public school rather than to the Caroline School, and then to their own Heder after school. About thirty-five children (including a few from the main community) ages six through fifteen, study in the Heder, where hours and subjects vary according to age. Older children are generally sent to yeshivot or girls' seminaries in England (Gateshead), Belgium, or Switzerland. In 1957, Machsike Hadas tried to open a yeshiva, sponsored by the Lubovich movement, but the school soon closed.[37]

80

The communal Talmud Torah for students not attending day school was replaced in 1971 by a series of
Weekend Institutes at a community campsite outside of
Copenhagen, called "Macabigarden." About half the
participants in such institutes came from the day
school and the rest from the general Jewish community.
The prototype of such seminars is that of the
California Brandeis Institute for Jewish Living. The
seminars were discontinued following a community
crisis in 1972 and were again inaugurated in 1975.

Bnei Akiva has its own study program. Several
public school students attend Bnei Akiva, but the
percentage of members attending the day school is
steadily increasing.

Judaica libraries in Denmark date back to the
reign of King Frederick III. Most have been
centralized in what is called Biblioteca Simonseneana,
in the Royal Library of Copenhagen. It has become one
of the most extensive Judaica and Hebraica libraries
in Europe and serves as the basis for the Chair of
Jewish Studies at the University of Copenhagen.[38]

Social Services

There are no special welfare programs, as there
are no poor Jews in Denmark who are not provided for
by regular Danish welfare programs.

The community supports three provisions for the
aged. One home, located in the section of Utterslev,
was constructed in 1967. In 1976, there were forty-
eight residents, twelve of whom were chronically ill
and thirty-six were elderly people unable to care
for themselves. The home is financed mainly through
the Municipality. The second home, called Meyers
Minde, is adjacent to the synagogue and caters to
about fifty residents requiring only partial care.
Part of the home's expenses are met by the
Municipality. In addition to the two Homes for the
Aged, next to the Community Center there is an

apartment complex for healthy senior citizens and for community employees, such as teachers, shochetim, shlichim, and so forth.

The Jewish Press

Danish Jewry publishes several Jewish periodicals. The community puts out a monthly magazine, called Jdisk Orientering, publishing local and world Jewish news. In 1975, the Jewish Youth Club and Jewish Student Club began publishing monthlies. Ajour, the Youth Club paper, is available to the whole community, while Jdisk Debat has a more limited circulation. The papers have come out with strong stands against the community establishment and one of the issues raised in the 1975 communal election campaign was censorship of the press. Bnei Akiva has published its own local newspaper for its members on and off for years. Hakoach also publishes a newspaper for its members. Israel, the quarterly of the Danish Zionist Federation, has an open subscription and is well received in both the Jewish and non-Jewish communities.

Many pan-Scandinavian Jewish organizations send their journals to members throughout Scandinavia. Thus, for example, B'nai Brith Nyt, published in Copenhagen, serves members throughout the Nordic countries.

Zionist and Other Bodies

The first Danish Zionist Federation was established in 1902, but was of interest to a very small circle. With the arrival of several Zionist leaders in Copenhagen during World War I, Zionist activity increased. In 1918, the Copenhaven office of the World Zionist Organization issued the organization's declaration of the Jewish people's objectives, both in Palestine and the Diaspora. From

82

1930 on the Copenhagen Jewish community newspaper began to publish articles about Palestine and Zionism, as well as about Hebrew and Yiddish culture. The Zionist organization was able to save many young Jews from the hands of the Nazis through its agricultural training scheme. About forty young Danes, Jewish and non-Jewish, left for Israel when Israeli independence was announced, joining volunteer military groups for foreigners.

Presently the Zionist Federation, numerically the largest Jewish organization in Denmark (with about 1,100 members) is considered a relatively inactive organization, although its members may be quite active in the community. The Zionist Federation leadership consists of an eight-member board elected annually at an open meeting of the Federation. The board is chosen on the basis of individual merits and interest, rather than by parties. Activities of the Federation include aliyah, membership drives, an information office and the Israel magazine. Annual Israel Independence Day celebrations are co-sponsored by the Zionist Federation and the community.

WIZO is the second largest Jewish organization in Copenhagen, numbering about eight hundred members. Its forerunner, the Jdisk Kvinderening (Jewish Women's Association), was a semi-Zionist organization formed in 1931, whose program emphasized study, social, and cultural activities. As a policy the Jewish Women's Association turned over one-third of its profits to WIZO. When a ban was placed on assembly during World War II, Association meetings were stopped but fund-raising efforts continued, providing supplies for refugees. With the flight to Sweden activities ceased entirely.

In January, 1946, WIZO was inaugurated, with Mrs. Meta Melchior its first president and constant mentor ever since. Although in the beginning mainly Zionist women joined, WIZO has become increasingly popular in all sectors of the community, regardless of age and background. In 1961, Aviv groups for young marrieds were begun and are now functioning on a geographical basis in ten neighborhoods.

Among WIZO activities are study groups, lectures, the annual Bible Day and annual bazaar. Danish WIZO is an affiliate of the Danish Zionist Federation, whose director is an ex-WIZO president. It is active in pan-Scandinavian WIZO.[39]

Zionist parties were active at various times but are presently inactive or weak. It is reported that groups of <u>Mizrachi</u>, <u>Avodah</u> and <u>Mishmeret Hatzeira of Mizrachi</u> are functioning, but that no group has more than fifty members.[40]

Danish Jewry has, for its size, a plethora of Jewish organizations and associations, ranging from the ultra-Orthodox <u>Machsike Hadas</u> to the Polish-founded <u>Bund</u>. Some are Yiddish speaking, some based around specific occupations, age groups or national origins, some are philanthropic, others, like the Jewish Bridge Club, are purely social. Many organizations meet at the Jewish Community Center, constructed in 1968.

One of the most prestigious clubs is B'nai Brith. The oldest chapter in Scandinavia, its activities include social and youth work. The present chairman of the Jewish community, elected in April, 1976, was president of B'nai Brith for several years. On the other hand, there are also many members who do not participate in other Jewish activities. B'nai Brith currently has 170 members.

The Jewish Sports Club <u>Hakoach</u> serves a membership of about five hundred youth and adults. It participates in national sports competitions and is an affiliate of World Maccabi.

Youth

The Jewish Students Club in Copenhagen has about thirty active members and a larger number of university students who sporadically attend functions. The club was organized in the early 1960's by the present chairman of the community. Since the arrival of the Israeli community shaliach in 1974, the club has taken on new life. Along with social activities, one of the club's main activities is the Hug Limud (study club) for the study of Hebrew and Judaism. This is a very important function, since the most active members and participants are Polish youth who have, at best, a rudimentary Jewish education.

The Jewish Youth Club currently has between 300 and 400 members, from the age of sixteen and up. Membership has remained stable since the end of World War II. The club is partly financed by the community.

Two youth groups that have recently disbanded are Moses, a short-lived teenage group for more traditional youth and Club David, a social club for teens, which disbanded in 1976. Perhaps the decline of Club David after fifteen years of existence can be attributed to the growth of Bnei Akiva, as well as to a lack of a clear raison d'etre.

Bnei Akiva is by far the most active youth movement in Denmark. In 1974 its membership doubled from about eighty to one hundred and sixty, and has remained steady ever since. As in other Scandinavian countries, the huge majority of members come from nonreligious homes. Partial credit, at least for the movement's recent growth is attributed to an increasingly active leadership and a continuous strengthening of Jewish commitment through education, religious and social experiences and Israeli orientation. In 1975, eighty Danish Bnei Akiva members attended the three week summer camp and ten participated in the Torah Seminar in Switzerland. An

85

increasing number of members attend the Caroline School and participate in the movement's educational activities, as well as in religious activities in the synagogue (choir, Torah readers, cantors). The group has a warm relationship with the Chief Rabbi, whose son was an active force in strengthening the movement.

Zeire Agudat Yisroel is a small youth group of the Machsike Hadas. Because most teenagers are sent abroad to complete their education, the group remains mainly an activities group for younger children. The youth from Polish refugee families have formed several clubs of their own.

In December, 1974, after much discussion a community shaliach was sent to Copenhagen, under the joint auspices and financial backing of the Jewish community of Copenhagen, the American Joint Distribution Committee and the Youth and Pioneering Department of the Jewish Agency. The Joint was especially amenable to arranging for such an appointment, for one of the shaliach's specific duties is to coordinate work in the Polish community. The shaliach set up a Central Youth Council, consisting of two representatives from each youth group, to coordinate activities and deal with the budget. In addition to his work with Jewish students and youth groups, and with the community of Århus, the shaliach has organized a Hug Ivrit (Hebrew club) for the adult community and a Talmud class for youth and adults. Recently he organized a monthly traditional Sabbath Eve dinner and cultural evening at the Jewish Community Center, attended by an average of fifty people of all ages, many of whom have not participated in other communal activities.

Until now youth groups have met at the Jewish Community Center, but the community has recently agreed to purchase a new Youth Center, where all youth groups can meet. The Joint and Youth and Pioneering Department will participate in funding the purchase.

Communal Finances

The community receives the proceeds of the Church Tax, a 1.85 percent tax calculated according to income and paid directly to the community. (Actually, this tax is substantially higher than the Christian Church tax.) Special arrangements are made for people unable to pay the full amount. In the 1930's the community was quite wealthy, and has since then used some of the interest from its capital; however, most of the money is in the form of legacies earmarked for specialized use and thus may not be operative today. Community members pay small fees for religious services, and dues and fund-raising drives increase the incomes of all organizations, but there are generally no extra fund-raising drives or appeals for community causes. The Board of Representatives decides all communal allocations.

From community records for the year 1972-1973 and 1973-1974 it seems that the financial situation of the community is weakening, in contrast to the financial situation of its individual members. In 1972-1973 the community just broke even with a surplus of DK 8,000. By the following year a serious deficit of DK 121,000 had developed. The community covered the deficit in two ways: by using money in the communal treasury (legacies and grants) and by taking out new loans.

Most of the communal funds are used for cultural purposes, including allocations to various organizations and institutions and for purposes of religious ritual.

In addition to the three main buildings owned by the community (the Main Synagogue, the Community Center, the Day School), the communal treasury owns property and receives funds contributed by individuals throughout the years. Total assets in 1975 were DK 12,086,000.

Table 2. The Communal Budget, 1972-73 and 1973-74[1]

	1972-73	1973-74
Community Income:		
Community Taxes	DK 1,611,000	DK 1,670,000
Community Grants	19,000	50,000
Sundry Income (Kashrut Certificates, etc.)	60,000	61,000
TOTAL	DK 1,690,000	DK 1,781,000
Community Expenditures:		
School and Culture	373,000	493,000
Cemeteries in Copenhagen	38,000	114,000
Cemeteries outide Copenhagen	7,000	3,000
Building at N.V. Konensg.	134,000	158,000
Old Age Home[2]	117,000	85,000
Main Synagogue	83,000	105,000
Ritual Affairs (kosher slaughtering, etc.)	113,000	119,000
Budget for Committee of Gabayim	250,000	294,000
Administration	281,000	290,000
Pensions	112,000	110,000
Special expenditures	50,000	34,000
Travel expenses and receptions	18,000	7,000
Interest payment on loans	28,000	38,000
Aid to refugees[3]	78,000	50,000
New Building	----	2,000
TOTAL	DK 1,682,000	DK 1,902,000
Final Statement:		
Expenditures	1,682,000	1,902,000
Income	1,690,000	1,781,000
TOTAL	DK + 8,000	DK -121,000

[1]Community records for 1972-1974, as recorded by Dov Levittan.
[2]Most of the expenses of the Old Age Home are covered by the municipality and state. The community furnishes only a small part of the funds.
[3]Mostly post-1968 refugees from Poland.

The community pays the salary of the Chief Rabbi and his assistant, when there is one. The Machsike Hadas supports its own rabbi, when it has one, but receives some community funds for its Heder.

The annual Magbit campaign starts off with a cultural evening for the community, during which the Chief Rabbi makes an appeal and contribution cards are distributed. The Israeli Embassy holds open houses for every professional group. An attempt was made to organize a Youth Magbit, but Bnei Akiva is the only youth organization currently participating. About fifty percent of the Jewish community contributes to the Magbit. Approximately DK 3,000,000 was raised in 1975. Special campaigns for non-Jews were held after the Israeli wars in 1967 and 1973.

Keren Kayemet Le Israel is very popular in Denmark. Collections were begun in 1933, and throughout intervening years several forests and woods have been planted in honor of the Danish people and their government. Trees are often planted in honor of non-Jews. All Keren Kayemet gifts are announced in the community magazine.

The Conference on Material Claims against Germany contributed a great deal of financial assistance in the reconstruction of Jewish life in post World War II Denmark. It provided funds for completely renovating the community synagogue in 1961 and contributed largely to building the Homes for the Aged and the Jewish Community Center.

Financial assistance given by the American Joint Distribution Committee and the Jewish Agency for Israel have already been cited.

Political Dynamics of the Jewish Community

The Board of Delegates in its present form was created in 1936, with the aim of democratizing voting privileges within the community. Previously, the Jews of East European origin had not been permitted to vote or hold office, and leadership was left entirely in the hands of old families. Two main factors precipitated the change: The East Europeans had become sufficiently acclimated to both the country and the Jewish community; furthermore, they were recognized as the major factor in curbing assimilation, because of their stronger Jewish commitment and culture. Second, in an atmosphere of rising Social Democracy in Denmark on the one hand and persecution of Jews on the other, it was unseemly that the Jewish community continue to be undemocratic.[41]

In the first new elections, held in 1936, six of those elected to the then twenty-one-member board were of East European background. Between 1936 and 1976, social integration between the two groups has become increasingly stronger, until today, Jews of both origins vote for and are represented in all party lists.

An examination of the party lists of the last twenty years shows that all agree on several major communal goals: community unity, a curb on assimilation, preference given to education and organizational activity, and identification with Israel. Differences in party platforms tend to be centered on religious philosophy or on personalities.[42]

Communal elections are a very strong issue in the community, especially because of the struggle for leadership between those who support the Chief Rabbi and those opposing him. In recent years campaign brochures have been brought out by the various party lists before elections and the community newspaper has been widely used for publicity purposes.

The usual community party lists are as follows: The Liberal List is traditionally supported by the old Danish families, who are generally liberal or atheist in religious adherence. Many families have served in community leadership roles for generations. The chairman of the community has often come from this list. Today, however, one finds a large number of Jews of East European origin in this party as well. The Traditional List is comprised mainly of members of the main synagogue, who may or may not be personally observant. Machsike Hadas sometimes has its own list and sometimes joins the Liberals. There are also non-ultra-Orthodox people who support the Machsike Hadas list. In 1968, young adults formed the first Youth List, based on a platform of reforms in favor of activating younger people in communal affairs. The Youth List employed modern propaganda and information techniques in the election campaign and scored a majority victory in the first elections; it has remained a vital force in the community ever since.

The period between 1972 and 1975 was one of crisis in Jewish community affairs and the 1975 elections reflected the consequences of the tension. 73 percent of eligible voters participated in these elections, a slightly greater number than in the previous one. Of the twenty member board selected, four of the delegates chosen represented a combined ticket of the Liberals and a religious group opposing the Chief Rabbi; six delegates represented the Youth List; five, the Traditional List of the synagogue; three, the Machsike Hadas; and two delegates from a special list set up to support the Chief Rabbi. (It has been suggested that 90 percent of this list would ordinarily have voted Traditional.)

The Board of Representatives is elected by the Board of Delegates. The seven representatives chosen bi-annually on a rotation basis of three or four per election, serve on the Board of Representatives for a term of four years. The chairman of the Board of

92

Representatives is called the Chairman of the community.

Until recently, all members of the Boards of Delegates and Representatives held important positions in Danish life, as prominent businessmen, lawyers, professors, politicians, and so on. This situation more or less changed in the 1960's, when much less emphasis was placed on this kind of status; the change reflects a general trend toward democratization and anti-intellectualism prevalent in Denmark today. Another major change has been the growing inclusion of younger people in leadership roles.

The first woman elected to the Board of Representatives was chosen in 1972, but women have served on the Board of Delegates for some time. One of the issues debated in the 1975 community elections was whether or not to grant women the right to vote in elections for the Committee of Gabayim for the synagogue.

It is extremely difficult to understand the flavor of Jewish life in Denmark without examining the status of the Chief Rabbi throughout the years, for in such a small community clashes between opponents and supporters of the incumbent Chief Rabbi tend to cause repercussions in all spheres of communal life.

Rabbi Abraham Salomon was appointed the first rabbi of the Copenhagen community in 1687. The Copenhagen rabbis of the nineteenth century opposed the Reform movement emanating from Germany and which grew more and more acceptable to a large segment of the Danish community. It was Dr. Abraham Alexander Wolff, Chief Rabbi of Denmark from 1828 to 1890, who united the various religious factions and gave a religious image, as well as an orderly administrative form, to the community. Much of the rabbi's thought concerned creating a synthesis between modern and traditional Judaism.

93

The first major communal rift over Chief Rabbis occurred in 1910, when Chief Rabbi Lovenstein, who had been appointed in 1903, was found unacceptable to the community because of his strictly Orthodox leanings. The rabbi had been given a life contract and well-defined powers, but the Board of Representatives nevertheless appointed another rabbi, a young Zionist with Conservative leanings, and entrusted him with authority which stood in violation of the Chief Rabbi's contract. Finally, in 1910, the community suspended the Chief Rabbi completely, going so far as to physically lock up his seat in the synagogue. A legal battle ensued, both in the Danish civil courts and between rabbinical authorities throughout Europe. In 1912, the Danish Supreme Court ruled in favor of the Chief Rabbi and the community was forced to pay him a considerable sum for breach of contract (he was paid more money than the community had collected that year in taxes).

The struggle between the Chief Rabbi and the community inevitably also became one between the two rabbis involved, but it was much more an issue in which part of the community had turned against the rabbi. During the two year court struggle, those members of the community who favored Rabbi Lovenstein formed their own minyan where he could pray. This group was the forerunner of the present Machsike Hadas congregation in Copenhagen. As a result, from its inception, Machsike Hadas has always joined in any fight against the community rabbis.

In the decades of the 1950's and 1960's another struggle developed when part of the community again turned against its Chief Rabbi, this time Rabbi Marcus Melchior. Rabbi Melchior was the first native-born Chief Rabbi in fifty years. (The first had been Rabbi David Simonsen, who had succeeded Rabbi Wolff.) Rabbi Melchior was one of the most popular personages in all of Denmark, constantly sought after because of his oratorical skills. In the unrest of pre-World War II days, Dr. Melchior wrote prolifically against the dangers of anti-Semitism. During the war he ministered to the spiritual needs of the Danish refugee community in Sweden. But after the war he preached that one cannot conserve hate, even against Germany. He preached this theme to both Jewish and non-Jewish audiences. When, therefore, in 1958, he was asked by George Duckwitz, the German Ambassador to Denmark (who had aided the Jews to escape to Sweden in 1943) to accept the Federal German Medal of Merit, he consented to do so. Large segments of the community could neither accept nor condone such an act and the Board of Representatives issued a statement deploring the Chief Rabbi's action. From this point on the rabbi ceased to be the combined social and religious power in the community and two distinct camps, pro-Melchior and anti-Melchior developed, with the result that part of the community automatically opposed any of the Chief Rabbi's actions.

In 1962, in the wake of a visit to Denmark by Israeli Prime Minister David Ben Gurion, in which the Prime Minister criticized assimilationist tendencies in Scandinavia and called for aliyah as the only means of survival, Rabbi Melchior issued a statement in which he expressed satisfaction with Danish Jewry, who were good citizens, and saw no conflict between their strong loyalty to Denmark and their devotion to Israel. Perhaps Rabbi Melchior would have felt less compelled to speak out had Ben Gurion's remarks not been prominently reported by the Danish news media. Rabbi Melchior's statement elicited strong criticism from the Danish Zionist Federation, which published a statement without the rabbi's knowledge in all newspapers and magazines which had printed the rabbi's statement.

Machsike Hadas joined the fray, accusing the rabbi of being lax in conversions and generally suspect because of his Conservative leanings. As the rows progressed, the community became wracked with dispute; letters were written to rabbis abroad and Danish newspapers carried a full account of the struggle. The dispute was finally brought to the Boards of Deputies and Representatives and Rabbi Melchior threatened to resign unless he were given a

95

public vote of confidence (which he received by a four to three majority of the Board of Representatives).

In 1972, the latest community crisis developing from conflict between a Chief Rabbi and the community occurred, this time with Chief Rabbi Bent Melchior (Rabbi Marcus Melchior's son) as protagonist.

Rabbi Bent Melchior had received his rabbinical ordination from the Orthodox Jews College in London and returned to Copenhagen in the late 1960's to act as second rabbi for the community. Those elements in the community who opposed the Chief Rabbi also found fault with his son, who, they thought, had been too influenced by his father. Nevertheless, Rabbi Bent Melchior became Chief Rabbi upon his father's death. Rabbi Melchior established an excellent relationship with the youth, who were often anti-establishment. He also, like his predecessor, has Conservative leanings, and recently accepted a vice presidency of the World Council of Synagogues of the Conservative movement.

Following the massacre of eleven Israeli sportsmen at the 1972 Olympics in Munich, memorial services were held in the Copenhagen synagogue. Conflict arose as to the form such a service should take and who should be present. After agreeing to inclusion of memorial prayers in the regular High Holiday service, the Chief Rabbi acquiesced to demands to hold a special memorial youth service. Moreover, he issued a statement to the Danish press concerning the massacre. Many community leaders felt the rabbi had no right either to act as spokesman for the community or put himself in a position where he might be thought to be its spokesman. Joining his opponents was the Machsike Hadas block, who always sided against the Chief Rabbis, this time complaining that he did not follow halacha in performing conversions. In addition, a large opposition block was composed of Jews socially, politically and religiously "liberal," who were offended at having internal Jewish disagreements once again blasted across the pages of the Danish press. These people believe that a Jewish community should definitely exist in Denmark, that it

96

should support a rabbi and carry out religious functions, but that it must not cause any public notice to be taken of it.

Nine members of the Board of Deputies supported the Chief Rabbi, and eleven opposed him. As the conflict grew, Rabbi Melchior tendered his resignation, which, in accordance with his contract, was to take effect a year later. The Chairman of the community, who was running for the Danish Parliament, also resigned. The battle raged for some time, until finally an Arbitration Board of three people, one selected by the Board of Representatives, one by the rabbi, and one jointly selected, was set up. Any future complaint should be taken to this body, which if it agreed, could censure the rabbi (but in practice this would hardly be likely, due to the composition of the board), but no other group would be granted the right to publicly censure.

The 1972 crisis affected almost every area of Jewish life in Denmark. New appointments to the communal boards were made. The editor of the community newspaper, who had taken a strong anti-Melchior stand, was replaced. Since 1972, a slightly higher percentage of Jews have opted out of community membership, or contemplated doing so; many were peripheral Jews to start with, but many others were young people who became disgusted with the pettiness of communal politics. The successful weekend seminars which had replaced the Talmud Torah were disbanded by the young leaders and teachers, as a sign of protest against the Board of Representatives, and remained inoperative for three years. Supervision of Jewish education was for a time taken out of the hands of the Chief Rabbi.

Since the 1975 elections, the majority of the Boards of Delegates and Representatives are pro-Melchior. The coalitions of party lists in 1975 clearly demonstrate the two camps and the division of loyalties within the community. A growing pro-Melchior force is the Youth List, representatives

97

of the young people as a whole, who generally support the Chief Rabbi.

Not everything in the community causes crises. An example of different factions working together is the united effort on behalf of Soviet Jewry. When Kosygin visited Denmark in 1972, a protest demonstration was held. It was agreed to begin the demonstration as a service within the synagogue, giving the occasion the official sanction of both the Chief Rabbi and the Board of Representatives, and then moving out into the streets. When a request was made to send a petition on behalf of Soviet Jewry to the Danish government, it was agreed that petitions should be presented by the Board of Representatives.

Following the Leningrad Trial a Danish Action Group for Soviet Jewry was inaugurated and a large official Danish Committee for Soviet Jewry was organized by the Chief Rabbi, with most, if not all, imortant members of Parliament represented.

Danish Jewry and Israel

Denmark extended de jure recognition to Israel on
July 7, 1950. Danes looked favorably upon the
establishment of a Jewish state and had, through the
Danish Red Cross and various other relief
organizations, aided Jewish refugees in transit to
Israel, but the Danish government withheld initial
recognition of the state, out of concern for the fate
of Palestinian refugees. The Israel Legation
in Copenhagen was opened in January, 1953 (until then
the Legation in Stockholm had represented all of
Scandinavia), and in 1961 the first ambassadors were
appointed. Leaders of the Social Democratic Party,
Denmark's leading political party, have always been
strong supporters of Israel, whether in the European
Common Market or the United Nations. High-ranking
officials have made several state visits in both
countries. Denmark remained one of the few countries
withstanding the pressures of the Arab oil embargo in
1973. Trade between Denmark and Israel has flourished
throughout Israel's existence.

It is true that recently there has been slightly
stronger support for the Palestinian Arabs.
Discussion is now taking place in Parliament, the
Government, and among the public on whether to allow
the Palestine Liberation Organization to open an
information office in Copenhagen. (The Danish Prime
Minister had promised President Sadat that one would
be opened.) The matter is being taken to the Danish
Supreme Court by a member of the Jewish community,
himself a politician.

The Jewish community in Denmark has reacted to
Israel with characteristic ambivalence. Danish Jewry
had developed along the lines of a religious
community, rejecting the national aspect of the Jewish
people in order to emphasize allegiance to Denmark.
Throughout its history, the Jewish community continued

99

to remain insular, although on several occasions it aided other Jewish communities in distress. Zionism took hold in Denmark only several years after the Russian Jewish immigration to the country. Not even the creation of the State of Israel moved the Danish Jews to question its loyalties. Thus, it is not surprising that while proud and happy at Israel's establishment, the Jews of Denmark have not been top contributors to Israeli causes, while they have been most generous in contributions to local charities. Together with the rest of Scandinavia, Denmark has produced a stream of aliyah, but mostly by young people associated with Bnei Akiva. However, it is felt that since the Six Day War Danish Jewry has experienced and expressed a much deeper interest in its connections to Israel and to World Jewry. Danish youth and adults have been vocal in their support of Russian and Arab Jewries. The Danish Jewish community joined the World Jewish Congress in 1975. Many Jewish as well as non-Jewish Danish youth have joined volunteer programs working on kibbutzim in Israel.

Summary

Jewish settlement in Denmark, dating from the early seventeenth century, is the oldest in Scandinavia. A formal community was recognized in 1657. The Jews assimilated well into the economic life of the country, often adjusting their occupations to economic demands of the times. Educational and cultural opportunities were open to them by the end of the eighteenth century and political freedom was granted within the following fifty years. The small Jewish community greeted its acceptance with loyalty and enthusiasm, and had so entered into Danish society that by the twentieth century, that it all but disappeared. The wave of Jewish immigration from Russia in the first quarter of the twentieth century re-established a vital Jewish community.

Denmark proved its loyalty to its Jewish citizens by showing Nazi Germany it would not tolerate ill treatment of its Jews. The Germans, on the other hand, exploited their humane treatment of Danish Jewry for several years. When finally the Jews were to be deported to Theresienstadt, almost the entire Jewish population was secreted off to Sweden by the Danish Resistance movement, with full support of the Danish government and citizenry. Following the war, the Jews were welcomed back to assume their place in Danish society.

The rate of intermarriage and assimilation remains high in the contemporary Danish Jewish community and poses a very real potential threat to the continued survival of Danish Jewry. The low incidence of anti-Semitism in Denmark strengthens the Jews' feelings of acceptance there.

The community is governed by an elected Board of Delegates and its Board of Representatives. Elections to these bodies are major community events, airing many underlying issues and disagreements between

101

various segments of the community. Religious life is directed by the Chief Rabbi, according to formally orthodox community ritual, although orthodoxy is not practiced by the majority of individuals. Nevertheless, there is a small ultra-orthodox segment of the community, preserving its own institutions. In recent years there has been an increase in interest shown in Jewish education and youth work. Zionist work continues, especially through the efforts of Danish WIZO, but Danish Jews continue to emphasize their primary loyalty to Denmark.

Communal activities are financed by a special "Church Tax" of 1.85 percent of taxable income and through fees for various drives and campaigns. The Conference on Material Claims Against Germany and, later, the American Joint Distribution Committee and the Jewish Agency for Israel have provided financial assistance for community projects. It is estimated that between 60 and 70 percent of the community participate in communal activities. The non-Jewish community also attends some community functions.

Years ago predictions were made, based upon intermarriage and birth statistics, that the Danish Jewish community could not continue to survive much longer, and yet today's community of eight thousand, with a growing commitment to Judaism on the part of at least some of its members, contradicts such pessimism. If a large percentage of the newly arrived immigrants from Poland, who comprise nearly one-fourth of the Jewish population, can somehow be channeled back to Jewish identification and involvement, the question of survival of Danish Jewry, would be positively answered.

THE JEWS OF NORWAY

Simcha Werner and Adina Weiss Liberles

Social and Historical Background

The first Jewish settlement in Norway dates back to about three hundred years ago.[1] However, in comparison to other Jewish communities of the diaspora, the Norwegian community is a relatively young one which began to develop as a community only at the end of the nineteenth century. In 1875, the Jewish population of Norway numbered only thirty-four, of whom seventeen lived in the capital city. In 1890, the number of Jews living in Norway reached 214, of whom 136 lived in Oslo. The period between the two World Wars was marked by the physical growth of the Jewish population and an increase in the scope of religious and social activities through various secondary organizations operating within the framework of communal roof organizations. However, the Oslo community (which is the largest Jewish center in Norway) suffered for many years from severe internal conflicts which constituted an obstacle to the organization of a united community capable of functioning as a community. The critical period of "community building" was thus marked by divisions and disputes. Only on the eve of World War II did the Jews of Oslo come to the realization that their continued existence as a religious and social minority required that the independent frameworks be abolished and that the community be organized on a unified basis.

The effect of the Holocaust on the Jewish community in Norway was ruinous. Some 760 Norwegian Jews -- about half of the population -- perished in the concentration camps. Those who succeeded in escaping from the clutches of the Nazi regime were forced to evacuate their homes and to flee the country. At the end of the war, the Jews who survived returned and, with the aid of the government, the Jewish community was reestablished by the granting of entry visas to Jewish refugees from other European countries. The positive attitude of the government and the sympathetic attitude of the Norwegian public as well as dynamic community leadership all contributed to the relatively speedy rehabilitation of the Jewish community. However, the economic situation of the community was very poor and its social composition heterogeneous, and, at the conclusion of the post-war period of recovery and rebuilding, the community found itself in a situation fraught with new dangers.

Norway today is characterized by a high level of religious freedom, the absence of anti-Semitism, and government and public support for the Jewish community. In this environment there exists a small Jewish community, lacking financial resources, free from any social hostility, whose members have only loose ties with its religious institutions, a community for whom the synagogue has only symbolic value. Such an environment is conductive to the development of a process of assimilation as well as of physical and cultural integration. In the absence of restraining mechanisms, the community finds itself in serious difficulties with regard to its chances for long-term survival.

The religious, social, and, to a certain extent, even the political behavior of the Jewish community and its institutions is affected to a considerable degree by the behavior of the surrounding Norwegian community. That is to say, general patterns of behavior of Norwegian society were adopted by the Jews and applied within the Jewish community itself.

This chapter deals primarily with the Jewish community in Oslo which, since the earliest Jewish settlement in Norway, has been the central and largest community in the country. Until World War II, there was limited Jewish settlement in several other urban centers. Only in Trondheim, whose Jewish community today numbers 120, was settlement renewed to the extent of forming a community.

The best and most detailed study of Norwegian Jewry is that of Oscar Mendelshon, dealing with the history of the Jews of Norway until World War II. This study, in Norwegian, is based on excellent documentation and contains abundant primary information. The information on the contemporary Jewish community in Norway is drawn from various articles in English, Jewish encyclopedias, reports of the Jewish community in Oslo and from the press -- in particular from the Jewish Chronicle. Interviews were conducted with members of the Oslo community living in Israel, primarily students, and in particular with the appointed rabbi of the community, Rabbi Michael Melchior. The first author of this chapter lived in Oslo for two years where he served as cultural coordinator of the local Jewish community.

The Christian religion penetrated into the Norwegian community relatively late (in the eleventh century) and, through the religious literature, the people of Norway were first acquainted with the Jewish world. In any case, until the seventeenth and nineteenth centuries, the history of Norwegian Jewry was linked to that of the Jews of Denmark. Norway was under Danish domination for four hundred years, from the beginning of the fifteenth century until 1814. During the period of union with Denmark, the economic, political and cultural systems of Norway were shaped by the Danish regime. The authority to enforce the laws and to implement the policies of the Danish government was granted to an inflexible and very powerful colonial bureaucracy.[2]

Danish Jews of Portuguese origin conducted trade with Norway in the latter half of the seventeenth century, visited Norway, and perhaps even settled there. During the reign of Christian V, the authorities continued to allow controlled settlement of wealthy Jews in Denmark. The new settlers were required to engage in commerce according to a fixed minimal quota and subject to the conditions noted

105

above. The authorities also ruled that any Jew entering the country had to possess a "letter of safe conduct" (leidebrev) by whose terms the bearer was responsible for his own self-protection. These restrictions allowed only a small number of Jews to enter the united kingdom, and even those who did were limited to the period of time set in the permit, for the purpose of conducting their business. Mendelshon cites evidence that Jews who attempted to enter Norway without a "letter of safe conduct" encountered a hostile attitude on the part of the police and were forced to leave the country.[3] Several Jews who settled in Norway during the eighteenth century did so by declaring their intention to convert to Christianity. This small handful in a short time were totally assimilated into Norwegian society.

With the Norwegian Constitution of 1814 continuing to deny the right of the Jews to settle in the country, the first half of the nineteenth century in Norway was marked by a protracted struggle by the liberals to achieve religious and social freedom for the Jews.

The political system that evolved in Norway is based on the constitution of May 17, 1814, which declared the independence of the state. The treaty of Kiel of that same year transferred the sovereignty over Norway from Denmark to Sweden. The Norwegians' unilateral declaration of independence led to a political conflict and to acts of violence, at the conclusion of which Norway was forced to recognize the union with Sweden. The Norwegian constitution was recognized by the Swedish crown and Norway in fact enjoyed semi-independence, remaining responsible for domestic affairs. Through a slow and continuous process, the powers of the Norwegian political institutions were extended, until Norway achieved full independence in 1905.

The Norwegian constitution of 1814, known as the "Farmers' Constitution" (because most of the members of the constituent assembly were farmers) was considered one of the most progressive constitutions

106

of its time. However, Article 2 of the constitution stated:

> The Evangelist-Lutheran Religion shall be maintained and constitutes the established church of the Kingdom. The inhabitants who profess the same religion are bound to educate their children in the same. Jesuits and Monastic orders shall not be tolerated. Jews are furthermore excluded from the kingdom.[4]

Among the members of the constituent assembly which adopted the constitution were a number of liberals who were opposed to the wording and the content of Article 2, but, in the end, the article was adopted as stated by an overwhelming majority. A member of the constituent assembly, Lauritz Weidemann, who actively supported the continued restrictions on the entry of Jews into the country, expressed his opinion as follows:

> The history of the Jews demonstrates that this nation was always rebellious and deceitful, and their religious philosophy . . . has led them to intrigues and to constitute a state within a state.[5]

This hostile attitude towards the Jewish issue resulted, on the one hand, from the belief that the Jews constituted a source of danger to state security. Several delegates to the assembly representing the military sector, stressed the security-political aspect of the controversy in a period of the struggle for independence and nation-building. On the other hand, this attitude also grew out of a tradition of religious intolerance which was reflected in the attitude towards Catholics. The rural population in Norway, especially during this period, was Puritan. Even today, the political behavior of the rural population is influenced by a strong system of religious values.[6] Samuel Abrahamsen[7] notes that this attitude resulted from imaginary images formed within the Norwegian population in general and within particularly influential political groups in the absence of real interrelationships between Jews and Norwegian society. The underlying objective of Article 2 was to prevent a "Jewish problem" in the future.[8] A member of the constituent assembly who in 1817 conducted a public debate with a converted Jew by the name of Glogou, a debate widely publicized in the press, explains the position of the assembly as follows:

> You may be a just man, you have not offended me, but your faith is of such a nature that it cannot harmonize with our form of government. It is as a Jew, not as a human being, that we have excluded you. I could name for you states where the Jews by the hundreds of thousands have been mistreated, murdered, expelled, and deprived of their properties. It is in these states that you have to complain about injustices; they do not apply to us. We have not deprived you of anything, we have not imposed on you any restriction, we have only provided for our own security.[9]

Article 2 of the Constitution was strictly observed in the period following 1814. Jews who tried to enter Norway without a letter of safe conduct were placed under arrest and expelled from the country under police guard.[10] Permits to settle were granted only to those who converted. In the 1830's, only a few Jews succeeded in obtaining temporary permits for limited periods of time in order to conduct their business.

In 1839, the Norwegian poet Henrik Wergeland began his personal struggle for the abolition of social and religious discrimination against the Jews, a struggle which aroused considerable controversy. Influenced by the ideas of the enlightenment and romanticism, Wergeland became the "poet of liberty,"[11] and the standard-bearer of humanism and of social and religious tolerance in Norway. Wergeland's struggle prompted the Norwegian parliament to deal with the

108

Jewish question three times until the required two-thirds majority was attained for amending Article 2 of the Constitution. A parliamentary committee in 1842 recommended that the restrictions on the entry of Jews into the country be continued as stated in the Constitution; of one hundred members of parliament, fifty-one voted for the continuation of the restrictions, forty-three voted against and six abstained. Those who voted for the continuation of the existing policy towards the Jews were the representatives of agriculture, senior officials in the civil service, jurists, clergymen, and representatives of the regional municipal government. The votes of the businessmen were divided. The representatives of the urban sector and of the "intelligentsia" supported the liberal approach towards the Jews.[12]

Wergeland and his supporters continued to strive for a change in the public image of the Jews.[13] Article 2 of the Constitution was again brought up for discussion before the Parliament in September 1845, with the Jewish issue occupying much of the attention of the Members of Parliament. The opponents raised various arguments: the underdeveloped economic state of the country did not allow the open immigration of new populations; the granting of any official license for the entry of Jews into Norway was likely to lead to a wave of Jewish immigration that would only aggravate the economic difficulties of the Norwegian economy and society. They also argued that it was irrational to allow the settlement of Jews in the country before they had been granted full civil rights. This time, too, the liberals failed to achieve a two-thirds majority for the amendment of the constitution. Only in 1851 was a large majority of ninety-three Members of Parliament against ten with two abstentions[14] achieved, leading to the amendment of Article 2 of the Constitution and the lifting of the restrictions on the entry of Jews into the country, an amendment which entered into effect through a Royal Proclamation sanctioned by the King on September 24, 1851.

109

Wergeland, the foremost standard-bearer in the struggle for religious and social liberalism in his country, died following a prolonged illness six years before the amendment was adopted by the parliament. His poems and essays serve as a commemoration of his struggle for the rights of the Jews in Norway.[15]

The fears of the formulators of the Constitution of a mass Jewish immigration to Norway were not realized in the period immediately following the amendment of the Constitution. According to government statistics, there were only fourteen Jews living in Oslo in the late 1870's, all of whom dealt in commerce.[16]

Until the 1880's, there was limited Jewish immigration, mainly from Denmark, Germany, and other countries of Central Europe. The low rate of immigration by Jews to Norway can be explained by their hesitancy to settle in a country which had in the past displayed a hostile attitude towards the Jews and which was characterized by a lack of Jewish communities and a backward economy. With the rise of anti-Semitism in eastern Europe and particularly in Russia and the beginning of the great immigration, Jews came to Norway as well. The following table presents the growth of the Jewish population in Norway from 1865-1920. Thus, the Jewish population of Norway increased six-fold between 1875 and 1890, and the Jewish population in Oslo increased during that same period eight-fold.[17] Since the beginning of Jewish settlement in Norway, the Jews have tended to congregate in the urban centers, particularly in the capital city, and this tendency has become a constant factor in Jewish settlement in the country.[18]

The Jews who arrived before the 1880's were relatively young, 30 to 40 years of age, and most of them were engaged in commerce. They tried to advance their affairs by advertising in the local newspapers.[19] The tendency of the Jews to engage in commerce and, as a result, to settle in the cities, is also reflected in the circumstances of Jewish settlement in the city of Drammen, some thirty kilo-

110

Number of Jews in Norway from 1865 to 1920

	1865	1875	1890	1900	1910	1920
Oslo	14	17	136	343	688	(852)
Bergen	2	8	18	24	40	?
Trondheim	–	–	27	119	188	?
Other cities	9	3	29	79	67	?
Rural areas	–	6	4	77	62	(188)
Total Jews	25	34	214	642	1045	1457
Total Jews in cities	25	28	210	565	983	1269
Percent	100	82.3	98.1	88	94.1	87.1

meters from Oslo: in 1865 there were six Jews living there; following a serious fire that broke out in the city in 1866 and paralyzed the economic and commercial life there, all the Jews left the city.

The number of Jews living in Oslo in 1890 was 136, most of them newcomers concerned primarily with establishing themselves economically. Religious ritual was maintained through independent unorganized frameworks; religious services were conducted in private homes and only on holidays could a minyan (quorum of ten) be assembled for prayer. Religious education for children was nonexistent. Families whose financial situation permitted sent their children to Denmark -- from where the older families originated -- for their religious education.[20] In the period between 1851 and 1891, therefore, there were Jews living in Norway but without a communal framework.

Before we describe the developments that led to the establishment of an organized Jewish community in Oslo, we should note an historical event which is important to understanding the network of

111

relationships between the Jews and the Norwegian community as a whole. In 1873, a Swedish Jew by the name of Josephson was appointed director of the Christiana theatre in the capital city. This appointment evoked a public protest which found expression in the slogan "Away with the foreigners." This public protest, however, was not an expression of anti-Semitism directed against the candidate's Jewishness but was rather a protest against foreigners in general. Recent studies have revealed that the Norwegians display little tolerance towards foreigners and new immigrants.[21] The reaction to the case of the Swede, Josephson, can perhaps also be explained by his Swedish origin, because of the mixture of inferiority and jealousy which the Norwegians felt towards the Swedish people. In any event, a Jew came under attack in Norway because he was an outsider. In the Josephson affair, the "intelligentsia" revealed a sympathetic attitude towards the appointment; special note should be taken of the position adopted by the student organization (which also actively supported the Jews in the period of Nazi rule) and by the well-known Norwegian writer, Björnstjerne Björnson (1832-1910). Björnson, who also strongly condemned the Dreyfus affair, supported the appointment of Josephson and his continued functioning as director of the theatre.

As the Jewish population of Oslo grew, the need for a collective organization for dealing with religious and social problems became increasingly apparent. In 1891, a "Jewish Community Committee" was set up for the first time, headed by the earlier immigrants from Western Europe. This committee was to prepare the groundwork for the establishment of an elected community organization. One year later an organization called the "Jewish Society of Christian" (the previous name of the capital city) was founded. In 1893, the name of the organization was changed to the "Mosaic Religious Congregation" (Det Mosaiske Trossamfund--DMT). This organization undertook the task of solving pressing religious problems such as hiring a religious teacher for the community, finding a shochet (ritual slaughterer), and setting up a

112

synagogue which would replace the makeshift places of prayer set up in private homes.

The economic situation of the members of the Oslo Jewish community at that period was poor, and it was therefore only natural that the organization itself should lack sufficient means to develop community services. In order to establish the synagogue the leaders of the community approached a number of wealthy Jews in Europe, but their request for funds was turned down and the construction of the synagogue was postponed until the 1920's. It should be noted that the Jewish immigrants to Norway from Western Europe were not wealthy (in contrast to those who came to Denmark and Sweden), not to speak of those from Russia and Eastern Europe who were even less well off. The community continued to be characterized by a lack of financial means until after World War II.

With the increased settlement of Jews from Eastern Europe and Russia, changes began to appear in the social composition of the community in Oslo. The new immigrants had stronger ties to religion than their predecessors. In the course of time, serious conflicts erupted between them and the old leadership, which led to splits within the community and to the establishment of separate communal organizations. The social heterogeneity deriving from a different economic position, a different political and social culture, and a different religious identification prevented unity of action and thought in the critical period of community building. Instead of establishing representative and active leadership institutions which could carry out overall community objectives and creating an integrated community which would mobilize its resources in a comprehensive manner in order to solve community problems and provide religious and social services, the community gave birth to particularistic organizations in competition and in conflict with one another.

Nevertheless, during this time the Jews did become used to belonging to a Jewish religious communal organization. Even when a group found it

113

necessary to withdraw from an existing organization, a new religious organization was immediately set up to accommodate the dissidents and to incorporate them in an organizational-communal framework recognized by the government authorities. It is worthwhile noting that this trend towards membership in a religious community is a fixed characteristic of Norwegian society.[22] Otto Hauglin writes on this point:

> It can be said that the bond of people with any religious community is emphasized and fixed in the sense that there is no defined group within the population the majority of which is located outside some religious community . . . . In historical perspective, the membership of people in a religious community is a constant factor in the Norwegian social structure.[23]

The first conflict within Norwegian Jewry emerged as a result of the demand by a group of new immigrants from Eastern Europe to establish a separate synagogue. The reason behind this demand was their desire to maintain a more religious form of communal life. The establishment of a second organization became unavoidable after the expulsion of several members from the DMT because of failure to pay taxes. In 1893, an organization called the "Jewish Congregation" (Den Israelitiske Menighed) was established, numbering at its founding fifty persons. This organization remained in existence until 1910.

In 1903, there were four separate and competing communal organizations functioning within the Jewish community of Oslo. The third organization, Adat Yeshurun, was established in 1901 but ceased to exist with the death of its leader Dr. Asckanaze in 1908. In 1903, another organization called the "Orthodox Jewish Congregation" (Israels Orthodoxe Menighed) was established but was dissolved one year later.

Aside from the DMT, the lifespan of the other organizations was short. Throughout the entire period, the DMT remained the largest and the primary

114

organization of the Oslo community and the only one which continues to exist today. One of the matters of dispute among the different organizations was that of burial in the cemetery owned and operated by the DMT. In 1917, a serious dispute broke out over the high burial fees which the DMT levied from families that were not members of the organization. The dispute was brought before the Norwegian court. The DMT and its leaders argued that since a third of the organization's members could not afford to pay the burial fees and these were covered by the organization, the operation of the burial services constituted a heavy burden on it.[24] This dispute led to the establishment of a new organization, also called the "Jewish Congregation" (Den Isralitiske Menighed--DIM), which continued to exist until 1939, further aggravating the factionalism and the rivalry within the community during the difficult interwar period. It should be noted that although a Jewish cemetery had already existed for several decades, only in 1914 was a burial society (Hevrah Kaddisha) established within the DMT headed by an administrative committee composed of five members including one woman. According to the regulations of the society, one of the members of the administrative committee also served on the community's Board of Representatives. The burial society operated to a large extent on a volunteer basis.[25]

In 1916, the DMT decided to build a synagogue. A general assembly of its members was convened for this purpose. From the very beginning of the DMT's organization, the "community assembly" had served as a democratic means for decision-making. The construction of the synagogue was concluded in 1920. It contained two hundred seats for men and one hundred seats in the women's section. A small building was erected adjacent to the synagogue to serve as a religious school (heder), as well as a ritual bath (mikveh). After the completion of the synagogue and the mikveh, negotiations were conducted between the DMT and the DIM for the use of the mikveh. In April 1921, a contract was signed permitting the women of the "Jewish Congregation" (DIM) to use the mikveh free

115

of charge with the expenses for its operation divided equally between the two organizations. In 1940, the mikveh was closed because of financial difficulties.

The poor economic situation of the Jewish community in Oslo was very apparent at this time. Particularly in the period prior to World War I, but afterwards as well, the DMT found it difficult to recruit paid employees in the field of religious services. The manpower resources of the local community were limited and it was necessary to recruit functionaries from other Jewish communities in Europe. Moreover, because of the difficult financial situation of the organization, the tendency developed to hire one man to fulfill most of the religious functions at the same time. Thus, in 1899, the organization signed a contract with a man by the name of Skrapolski to serve as cantor, ritual slaughterer, circumciser, and teacher, while also being responsible for the sale of kosher meat and for burials.[26] The evidence cited by Mendelshon on the hiring of functionaries reveals that during this period the DMT held a strict and inflexible attitude towards those who held paid jobs within the community.

The organized community placed the primary emphasis on meeting physical religious needs and then on the establishment of a synagogue, which would serve both as a spiritual center and as a religious and social focal point. The role of the rabbinate and that of education were given only secondary importance. In 1915, pressure was brought to bear on the DMT leadership to engage a community rabbi. Dr. Chaim Rosenberg was chosen for this post, also serving as teacher in the heder and preparing the boys for bar mitzvah. In 1920, he was compelled to leave the community and the post of rabbi remained unfilled for ten years, until 1930.

Between 1910 and 1917 the DMT was the only organization which continued to function, and it grew considerably during this period through the affiliation of members of those organizations which had ceased to exist. During this time, secondary

116

organizations were established which functioned independently, such as the Jewish Youth Society (established in Oslo in 1909 and in Trondheim in 1917), a welfare organization and a mutual aid society (established in Oslo in 1906), a women's organization (in Oslo in 1913 and in Trondheim in 1919), and a Zionist organization (in Oslo in 1912). At first the Zionist organization embraced only a small number of members and its activities were limited. Oscar Mendelshon notes that in 1927, when the Board of Representatives of the DMT decided to register the organization in the "Golden Book" of the Jewish National Fund, it met with serious criticism on the part of the members of the community.[27] Moreover, when in 1929 the DMT Board was invited to participate in the founding of the Jewish Agency in Zurich, it did not receive the authorization of the community members.

During the 1920's, expressions of anti-Semitism began to appear, but their effect on the society and on public opinion was small. In 1909, a radical national movement was established which from 1916 on published a journal called Nationalt Tidskrift, in which anti-Semitic articles appeared regularly. During World War I and after the Russian Revolution, several rightist newspapers published articles derogatory of the Jews, accusing them of having caused the Russian Revolution and of stealing the world's wealth. Such subjects as the Balfour Declaration also served as cause for anti-Jewish attacks in these circles.

The shocks caused by World War I and the attacks against Jews in Poland and Russia led to closer ties between the DMT and the DIM, and to a joint appeal to the government to support the Jewish cause. The recognition of the need to unite in joint action increased in direct proportion to the frequency of the pressures to which the Jewish community in Norway was subjected. The public debate on the prohibition of Jewish ritual slaughter in Norway, which reached its climax in the latter half of the 1920's, also led to a closing of ranks between the two rival organizations

117

in Oslo. The public debate on ritual slaughter began
in Norway in 1890. In July 1926, the Norwegian
parliament passed a law prohibiting Jewish ritual
slaughter, which entered into effect in the beginning
of 1930.[28] The motivation behind this law was not
anti-Semitic but rather pressure from groups
protesting cruelty to animals. The "intelligentsia"
defended the Jews' right to freedom of religion.
Special note should be taken of Fridtjof Nansen, the
noted explorer, who argued that a country which wants
to grant religious freedom to religious minorities
cannot selectively and arbitrarily prohibit a
particular ritual practice of any religion.[29] In
1937, a humanitarian organization named after Nansen
was established in Oslo, with branches in Europe, to
deal with the problem of displaced persons, both Jews
and non-Jews.[30]

The rise of the Nazis to power in Germany led to
an increase in anti-Jewish activity in Norway as well.
The Norwegian Nazi Party was founded in 1933 and
published a newspaper entitled Free People. Other
newspapers having extreme rightist and anti-Semitic
leanings began to appear in the 1930's in several
major cities. In 1938, Fronten, a newspaper which had
begun publication in Oslo in 1932, called for the
expulsion of all Jews from Norway and for a ban on
their entry into the country.[31] Exstrablad called on
its readers to impose an economic boycott on Jewish
businesses. In Bergen, Samarbeid called for the
creation of a "free people" without a Jewish
minority.[32] The situation in other cities was
similar. Towards the end of the 1930's, caricatures
and indictments were pasted on the windows of Jewish
businesses. The influence of these actions on
Norwegian public opinion was minimal. Moreover, the
government and the political parties as well as the
major newspapers strongly supported the Jewish cause.
The expressions of anti-Semitism in Norway itself as
well as the political developments in Europe prompted
the two Jewish organizations in Oslo to unite. On
September 1, 1939, the day of the outbreak of World
War II, the unification of the two organizations went
into effect.[33] Thus there came to an end fifty years

of factionalism which had sapped the strength of the community.

In 1940, when Norway was conquered by Nazi Germany, there were 1,700 to 1,800 Jews living in the country. This number included some two hundred stateless refugees who had arrived in Norway upon the outbreak of the war. The German occupation government immediately imposed restrictions and prohibitions against the Jews, and in May 1941, the Nuremburg laws were extended to Norway. As a result, Jews were dismissed from government institutions and their right to engage in the liberal professions was revoked. In October-November 1942, 770 Jews were sent to extermination camps in Germany, of whom only twelve survived and returned after the war. An additional twenty Jews were killed in Norway itself during the course of the war, some of them shot to death. Throughout the war, the public displayed a sympathetic attitude towards the Jews, particularly the Norwegian student organization which demonstrated against the policy of Quisling's puppet government. The Norwegian Church also protested the hostile attitude towards the Jews. With the help of the Norwegian underground, some 930 Jews escaped to Sweden. This action was carried out with the help of the Norwegian Lifeboat Society. Only a few Jews managed to survive by hiding from the Nazi authorities in Norway itself.

Immediately after the war, the Jewish exiles who had survived began to return to Norway and were faced with the challenge of rehabilitating themselves as individuals and of rebuilding the community as a social framework. In September 1945, the community already numbered approximately 500 people (125 men, 250 women, and the rest children). The Norwegian government adopted a policy of goodwill, and in order to rehabilitate a community half of which had perished in the Holocaust, allowed 1000 new Jewish immigrants to settle in the country. The Norwegian immigration laws had always been rigid, and this decision in which the government circumvented its own laws served to demonstrate it goodwill towards the Jews. Another humanitarian gesture on the part of Norway was the granting of entry visas to seriously ill Jewish immigrants who had been rejected by other countries. The Joint Distribution Committee played an important role in the absorption of these immigrants. The Joint also helped the Jewish community organize a program of social activity and medical care for the rehabilitation of the new immigrants and even prevailed upon the authorities to grant them the status of "war casualties" and thus be eligible to receive government aid.

Some 700 Jews came to Norway under this program, but about half of them later emigrated, mostly to the United States and Israel. During the first five years after the war, the Jews worked primarily towards their own rehabilitation and the rebuilding of the community organization and institutions. In 1949, Dr. Zalman Aronzon was appointed rabbi of the Oslo community. Dr. Aronzon, who had served for many years in public positions in the Jewish communities of Finland and Sweden, did much to further the religious, social and cultural rehabilitation of the Jewish community in Oslo. However, the supply of kosher meat remained problematic as a result of the policy of the Ministry of Agriculture and the veterinary services which prohibited the importation of meat from outside the country for fear of the spread of hoof and mouth disease. The supply of kosher meat to the Jewish community was only renewed in 1951.

Norway also aided Jewish refugees indirectly by serving as a transit station from other countries, particularly for children whose rehabilitation was begun there on their way to Israel. In November 1949, a plane carrying twenty-five children from Tunisia destined for Israel crashed in Norway. A year later, a non-Jewish group raised a million kroner for the purchase of fifty prefabricated homes which were set up in Kfar Yanuv near Netanya, most of whose inhabitants were immigrants from Tunisia. The name of the village was changed by the residents themselves to "Kfar Norvegia."[34] It is worthwhile noting that the Norwegian labor party took an active part in organizing this project.

In September 1952, the community celebrated both 100 years since the beginning of Jewish settlement in Norway and the sixtieth anniversary of the founding of the DMT, with the participation of representatives of the government, the political parties and the church, as well as descendants of the poet Wergeland.[35]

In the mid-1950's, the Jewish community in Norway numbered roughly one thousand people of whom 700 lived in Oslo, 150 in Trondheim, and the remainder scattered throughout the country.

Several months after the end of the war and the return of the Jews to Norway, a Board of Representatives was elected in Oslo headed by Harry Koritzinsky, who continued in this position until 1975. Koritzinsky's contribution to the rehabilitation of the community was decisive. Since the war, the decision-making process of the community has been characterized by a tendency towards centralization. The Board of Representatives has accumulated considerable political power over the community it represents, power which grew as the leadership proved itself in dealing with the important problems of community rehabilitation. The success of the Board of Representatives in its contacts with the authorities also helped to strengthen its status and power.

The Community Today

The number of Jews in Norway today is estimated
at about 900 persons, of whom about 750 live in Oslo
and its suburbs and in the small cities nearby, and
some 120-150 live in Trondheim. A small number of
Jews live in other cities throughout the country.
According to government statistics, there were in 1973
a total of 873 people who adhered to the Jewish
religion.[37] Ninety-seven percent of the entire
Norwegian population is affiliated with the state
church. There are eleven other officially recognized
religious sects, but the total number of people who
did not belong to the state church in 1973 was only
115,119. The percentage of Jews that year among this
group was thus 0.8 percent, while the percentage of
Jews in the Norwegian population as a whole was only
0.02 percent.[38] In other words, the Jews constitute a
very small religious minority whose presence in the
society as a whole is not felt. Moreover, because of
the complete integration of Norwegian Jewry in the
society and economy of the country, as well as in its
institutions, government and otherwise, they cannot be
viewed as a social minority.

The fact that Norway is a state with a democratic
government and a free society can explain the
sympathetic attitude of both the government
institutions and the public at large towards the Jews.
The Norwegian government, the political parties, the
church and the press have come out strongly against
manifestations of anti-Semitism. In 1959, when
swastikas appeared in many countries throughout the
world including Norway, the government took a strong
stand and imposed the penal code against racial and
ethnic incitement. In 1974, a neo-Nazi party was
formed which called for the expulsion of Norwegian
Jews to Israel. This aroused a public uproar and the
party was outlawed by the government. During the
pre-World War II period, anti-Semitism had been
confined to a small minority in Norwegian society

123

which adopted radical right-wing ideological tendencies under the influence of German Nazism.[39]

The physical growth rate of the Jewish community in Norway is negative. The natural growth rate is small and is estimated at less than one percent. Data published by the Board of Representatives in Oslo indicate that in 1975 there were six births and nine deaths there. From interviews which we conducted, we learned that at least 50 percent of the marriages of members of the community are mixed marriages. Many Jewish families who fear that their children will marry non-Jews encourage them to go and study in larger Jewish centers. They are sent to Stockholm, to Copenhagen, to London, and to a certain extent also to Israel. There are in Israel today about ten Jewish students from Norway. The rate of immigration of Jewish families from Norway to Israel is small. A small number of singles have immigrated to Israel, and there is at present a gradual trend of emigration of Jewish families from Norway, primarily to Denmark.

The rate of mixed marriages in the Jewish community of Norway is lower than that in Sweden and Denmark. This can be explained by the fact that those members of the Norwegian community who arrived after the war from the countries of Eastern Europe still maintain stronger Jewish ties. However, because it is a smaller community than those of Sweden and Denmark, mixed marriages constitute a more serious threat to its continued existence. Thus, in Trondheim, the community has already begun to disintegrate because of the high rate of mixed marriages and the departure of families and youth. The synagogue of the Trondheim community was sold in 1972 as a result of the decreasing number of tax-paying members in the community organization and the inability of the community to meet the maintenance costs. Social organizations and especially women's organizations are still active in the city. The Oslo Jewish community faces similar threats.

Communal Organization and Finance

Following the dissolution of the communal organization in Trondheim several years ago, there is today only one communal organization functioning in Norway, the DMT--the Oslo community. In January 1976 the membership of the Oslo organization was 353, representing only 50 percent of the Jews living in that city. This number is in a constant state of flux, whether because of the emigration of families and youth to other countries or because of the constant exclusion of families because of non-payment of taxes. In 1975, for example, three members emigrated, seven were expelled because of non-payment of taxes, and 19 members joined the communal organization. The latter were for the most part former members who were reinstated or people who had not previously been interested in joining the organization.[40]

The Board of Representatives is the representative body of the community and is responsible to the official authorities in matters of community protocols, the registration of births, marriages and deaths, and the administration of religious life in the synagogue and schools. The Board of Representatives is elected for a period of three years by the tax-paying members of the community. The Board is composed of five members representing in general the social and economic elite of the Jewish community. Although the elections are democratic and "general meetings" are periodically conducted, the process of decision-making by the community leadership seems to be in the hands of a small group. The turnover of the elected representatives is small. The previous chairman of the Board, Harry Koritzinsky, served, as noted above, in that capacity for thirty years, acquiring considerable power in the community.

125

Democracy finds expression in the written regulations of the community, but is not fully realized in practice. It is interesting to note that this argument has been voiced by a number of Norwegian scholars with regard to the Norwegian system of government. Professor Johan Galtung notes that such a tendency is characteristic of the various organizations of Norwegian society, including its government.[41]

Until recent years, leadership was in the hands of the older members of the community. Since the early 1970's, however, there has been a tendency to increase the representation of the younger members, but in general they play a more active role in the leadership of the secondary organizations affiliated with the DMT.

The communal leadership of Oslo suffered a serious setback at the end of 1969 when the Norwegian government expressed a willingness to grant immigration visas to Jews from Eastern Europe on the condition that the Jewish community would be responsible for their absorption. The leaders of the community did not greet this plan favorably, and they were supported in this by a considerable portion of the veteran community. This issue aroused sharp dispute within the community. Strong opposition to the policy of the Board of Representatives was raised among the youth and students, led by the rabbi of the community who enjoyed considerable support and popularity within this sector. Members of the community who had come to Norway after the war were also opposed to the policy of the Board of Representatives. However, since the power and influence of these groups (the students and the new immigrants) is limited, it was ultimately decided not to implement the plan. In opposing this plan, the leaders of the community were giving voice to their fears that such an influx would constitute an economic burden on the community, and that the immigrants might possess religious ties that would not conform to the overall character of the community which is basically non-religious. This crisis undermined the status of

126

the old leadership and led to the introduction of younger members into the community organization.

It has already been noted above that both in its early stages and in the interwar period the Jewish community of Oslo lacked financial means. Today, while a small number of families have achieved financial wealth, the economic cross-section of the members of the community is middle class, and the economic status of those who arrived after World War II is even lower. Since the community is small, the Board of Representatives can assess the income of the members of the organization and determine the families' membership dues as well as the level of their contributions to the Keren Hayesod-Israel United Appeal accordingly. Since the community lives within a welfare state, the community organization is freed from dealing with welfare problems among its members. Moreover, as a religious community officially recognized by the authorities, it receives financial support from the government and the local authorities. In 1975, government support reached NKr 45,492 (Norwegian kroner), or about $10,000, representing 12 percent of the community's expenses for that year.

The income of the communal organization from membership dues in 1975 was NKr 225,860 ($50,000). That same year the expenses of the community were NKr 360,138 ($80,000), that is to say, the tax payments covered 62 percent of the expenditures. The communal organization suffered that year from an operational deficit of NKr 30,850 ($6,850), which was covered by various funds available to the organization. The operational and maintenance expenses of the community increase year by year, resulting in reductions in expenditures on culture, education, and Jewish social activities. Today the community employs a cantor and a rabbi, Michael Melchior. The total expenditure for paid functionaries amounted to NKr 57,000 or 16 percent of the total expenses for 1975.

From these data we learn that the financial situation of the DMT does not allow it to maintain a network of religious, cultural and social services capable of meeting the community's needs. The wealthy members of the community, who are few in number and pay high taxes, cannot by themselves supply the organization with sufficient funds to broaden its activities, while the raising of membership dues is liable in the long run to drive many away from membership in the organization. This situation constitutes a threat to the continued existence of the Jewish community in Oslo.

Religious Life

From the very beginning of the organized community in Oslo, insufficient attention has been given to the role of the rabbinate and of religious instruction, and there were considerable gaps in the filling of these functions. Between 1960 and 1968, the Oslo community remained without spiritual leadership. In 1968, the community hired a young Orthodox rabbi of Swedish origin who had completed his rabbinical studies in Jerusalem. He enjoyed considerable support in the younger circles of the community and tried to take an active part as well in the secular decisions of the community, an attempt which was not welcomes by the Board of Representatives. About a year and a half after he took office, a dispute broke out between him and the Board and his employment was suspended. The community remained again without a spiritual leader until 1975. In that year the community signed a contract with Rabbi Michael Melchior (born in 1954). According to the terms of the contract, the community was to finance his studies for a period of up to four years. Before assuming his position full time in 1979, he came to Oslo only for the high holy days. Since the rabbi usually serves also as teacher in the higher classes of the heder and as coordinator of the religious study groups for adults, those activities suffered in the interim.

The filling of the position of rabbi has always presented a serious problem, not only from the

128

financial point of view. In the period following World War II, the Board of Representatives sought to appoint an Orthodox rabbi who could speak one of the Scandinavian languages so that he would be acceptable to the community and to his students in the heder and the study groups.

The community synagogue in Oslo is officially Orthodox. All those who have served there in the capacity of rabbi have been Orthodox, and it seems to be the intentional policy of the community to maintain Orthodox life within the framework of the synagogue. However, it can be stated with certainty that the members of the community are not Orthodox. The interviews we conducted reveal that only a small number of families observe kashrut and the Sabbath. Throughout the week no services are held in the synagogue, and the Sabbath evening and morning services are attended by the older members of the community only, with the number of worshipers not exceeding twenty. Only on holidays and particularly on the high holy days is the synagogue full. It appears that the Jews of Oslo endow the synagogue with only a symbolic value of identification, unity, and the continued existence of the community (the synagogue was not damaged during the period of Nazi occupation and the Jews of Oslo emphasize this). The Norwegian Jews tend to maintain their Jewish life outside the synagogue and even outside the community center. They prefer to conduct activities within the framework of Bnai Brith, WIZO, and the adult study groups in private homes. This may perhaps reflect a trend within Norwegian society as a whole. Otto Hauglin notes that the Norwegian religion is a private religion which is conducted outside the church institutions:

It appears that the Norwegians view religion as possessing a social rather than a religious function. For a large segment of the Norwegian population, the church constitutes an important symbol of stability.[42]

129

Jewish Education and Youth

Regular Jewish education is conducted in the heder located in the community center adjacent to the synagogue. There are six classes in the heder for children between the ages of seven and twelve, with each class meeting twice a week. The language of instruction is Norwegian, but the students acquire a technical reading ability in Hebrew. During the last ten years, the cantor has also served as teacher in the lower classes of the Hebrew school. He teaches by the outdated method used in the classical heder. One of the serious problems of the school and of Hebrew and Jewish education in the community is the lack of continuity in instruction and the lack of qualified and experienced teachers. The gaps in the filling of the position of rabbi has also disrupted instruction in the higher classes. The community is forced to make use of visiting teachers, mostly from among the few Israelis studying in Norway. In most cases they, too, lack exerience and a pedagogic background. In 1975, three teachers were employed by the school in addition to the cantor-teacher, including one Israeli. For some reason the community leadership does not seek th aid of the Zionist Organization in employing schlichim as teachers. In 1975, there were some fifty students enrolled in the six classes, but there was a sinificant drop between the spring and fall semesters. With only thirty students enrolled in the fall, they were divided into four classes instead of six.

The adult study groups for men and women separately (on a social rather than religious basis) meet with the rabbi or an appropriate substitute is available. Today there is a group of forty men who meet once a week in what a known as the "Jewish Forum." Such activities are held in the homes of the participants and fulfill as much a social as a religious function.

The only youth organization active in Norway is Bnei Akiva, which serves as an important nucleus for

130

social and Zionist activity among the youth of the Oslo community. There is also a Jewish student organization, but, because of the small number of Jewish students studying in Norway, it does not play a significant role in the community. (We noted above the tendency in recent years for youth of college age to go to other countries to study.) The Jewish student organization in Norway is affiliated with the World Union of Jewish Students.

The Jewish youth in Norway in affiliated with the Scandinavian Jewish Youth Federation (SJUP), which holds joint social activities through conferences, summer camps, seminars, etc.

Social Services

The Jewish community center in Oslo was built in 1960 adjoining the synagogue. It houses the school and serves as a meeting place for Bnei Akiva and the student organization (whose activity is limited). The general "community meeting" and other community celebrations are also held there. The adult study groups and meetings of the B'nai Brith are conducted in private homes. There are two apartments in the community center, one for the cantor and one for the rabbi's family. It also houses the kosher meat store, which is open once a week. Unlike the Jewish community centers in Sweden and Denmark, the community center in Oslo does not have an "open door policy." It is open only for classes in the heder, for Bnei Akiva activities, or for other organized activities. In order to increase its income, the community rents out the hall of the community center to a non-Jewish bridge club and dance school.

The community owns a house in Baerum, which serves as a center for both youth and adults, especially during the summer vacation. In the summer of 1975, for example, a summer camp was organized there for eighteen children of the community, as well

131

as a Jewish pan-Scandinavian youth seminar. The B'nai Brith lodge in Oslo was founded in 1952 and its membership is composed primarily of academicians and members of the liberal professions. It enjoys a position of prestige within the community. The WIZO organization in Oslo has 200 women members and the Trondheim organization has forty, and in both cities the organization is very active.

Summary

Norwegian society, which displayed at the outset a negative attitude towards Jewish immigration, has in the course of time developed an attitude of tolerance, openness, and sympathy towards the small Jewish community which constitutes a very small minority in the society as a whole and is well-integrated into the economic, social and professional life of the country. A paradoxical situation has emerged, however, threatening the continued existence of the Jewish community. This situation is aggravated by the small size of the community and the meagerness of its resources, which do not allow for the provision of proper religious and cultural services that could increase Jewish consciousness, particularly among the younger generation. This combination of circumstances accelerates the process of assimilation of the community and threatens its continued existence even in the near future.

The identification of the Jews with Norway and its society and their integration within the society is high. The Jewish community has adopted patterns of religious and social behavior characteristic of the society at large, such as: the view of the synagogue as a symbol and the creation of a private religion, the adoption of patterns of leadership which are democratic in theory, individualism, and a negative attitude towards foreigners.

The Jewish community of Norway, which rapidly rehabilitated itself after the holocaust and lives in an environment of tranquility and prosperity, is in fact moving towards extinction and degeneration.

THE JEWISH COMMUNITY OF FINLAND

Adina Weiss Liberles

Historical Perspective

Until 1809 Finland was under the sovereignty of
the kingdom of Sweden and Jewish settlement was
forbidden there. When the country became a grand
duchy of the Russian Empire in 1809, Czar Alexander I
declared all existing Swedish laws valid, including
those against the Jews. However, many Jews from
Poland and Lithuania who had been kidnapped as
children by the Russians and forced to serve in the
Russian armny for twenty-five years served in the
Russian garrisons in Helsinki and Vyborg. Upon
completion of their army service, these Jews (called
"Cantonists," after the canton military schools) were
permitted to settle wherever in the Czar's dominions
they had ended their service. Nevertheless,
opposition to Jewish settlement was very strong on the
part of Finnish Christians, who promulgated a series
of restrictions on place of settlement, occupations,
and travel. Jewish children were permitted to live
with their parents in Finland only until they came of
age.

In 1872, two members of the Finnish Parliament
raised the issue of continuance of such restrictions.
Although the Parliamentary motion was opposed, the
debate continued in the Finnish press through the
1880's. Finally a law was passed in 1889, permitting
Jewish residence in Helsinki, Turku and Vyborg.
Approximately one thousand Jews resided in Finland at
that time.

Conditions improved in the twentieth century.
The emerging Finnish socialist movement symphathized
with the Jewish cause. Permission to build a
syngagogue in Helsinki had been granted in 1865 but it
was not until 1905 that the community was able to

135

raise the funds necessary to build one, on land donated by the municipality. The question of Jewish settlement was again raised in Parliament in 1909, where it was decided to abolish the restrictions against Jews. The Russian government, however, delayed ratification of the bill for the remainder of the time Finland remained under its dominion.

Once independence was received in 1917, Jews were granted full civil rights. The Jewish population had increased to two thousand as a result of immigration of Jews fleeing the Russian Revolution. For some, Finland was intended as a transit stop in a journey to the West. Restrictions on higher education were repealed in Finland and many Jews began studying for the liberal professions. While most Jews continued in the clothing and textile trades, the only occupations permitted them as Cantonists, others went into industry and forestry.

Jews fought in the Finnish army, both in the Finnish-Russian War of 1939-1940 and during World War II, when Finland was an ally of Germany, thus creating the paradox of Jewish officers serving alongside the Nazis. The Finnish government withstood all German pressures to enforce anti-Jewish legislation of any kind within its borders. A group of one hundred sixty non-Finnish refugees found refuge in Sweden for the duration of the war. Another group of fifty refugees from Austria and the Baltic States were to be deported but when news of the extermination of the first transport of eleven Jews reached Finland, Marshal Mannerheim and the Finnish government refused to continue the deportation. Contained in the peace treaty between Finland and the Allies in 1947 was a prohibition of racial discrimination, and thus the Jews once more enjoyed full civil rights under law.[1]

The Contemporary Jewish Community

In 1949, there were an estimated 1,700 Jews in Finland, most of whom belonged to the Jewish communities in Helsinki (one thousand members), Turku (three hundred members), and Tampere (fifty members). Approximately three hundred Jews in Finland were pre-World War II refugees; the rest were descendants of the Cantonists. More recent population figures vary slightly. The American Jewish Year Book for 1962 listed an estimated population of 1,500 Jews out of a general population of 4,500,000, with 1,100 members in the Helsinki Jewish community, 350 in Turku and fifty in Tampere, and an additional 250 Finnish Jewish citizens living abroad. Based on 1968 figures, the Encyclopedia Judaica estimated the Jewish population at 1,750, with approximately 1,330 Jews living in Helsinki; but the American Jewish Year Book, 1974, estimated the figure at 1,200 Jews in all Finland and only 875 in Helsinki for the year 1973, and the latter figures correspond with personal estimates.[2] Many Finnish Jews continue to live abroad and retain membership in the Finnish Jewish community.

The Jews are continuing in their occupations in the textile and clothing industries, however, more young Jews are becoming doctors, lawyers, engineers, industrialists and foresters than at the end of World War II.

Once Jews received equality in Finland, anti-Semitic attitudes against them, mainly on the part of conservative clergy, vanished. Preceeding World War II, a Finnish Fascist party existed, which carried on both anti-Jewish and anti-government propaganda, but the movement never gained in popularity. One of the articles of peace agreed upon between Finland and the Allies in the war called for a prohibition on any racial discrimination. From then on Jews once again enjoyed all civil rights and have

137

suffered from no overt manifestations of anti-semitism, although occasionally newspaper articles with anti-Semitic overtones appear. It has been suggested[3] that many more manifestations of philo-Semitism are to be found in Finland than the opposite. But a certain amount of social discrimination is felt by Finnish Jews, manifesting itself as a prejudice or stereotype about the Jews, who stand out in their appearance. Many Finns would object to their children marrying non-Lutherans (whether they be Jews, Swedes, or Gypsies).

No statistics have been published on intermarriage, but there are estimates that about half the Jewish population marrying today intermarries, and that the rate is rising, perhaps because children of mixed marriages are more likely to marry out than I children of two Jewish parents. [4] More than half the non-Jewish partners of mixed marriages convert, but often such families are not active in the community. Six years ago conflict arose in the community as to whether the Jewish partner of a mixed marriage where the other partner did not convert should be given a leadership role in a Jewish organization, in this case, the Youth Organization. The club almost split over the issue, until it was finally decided that partners of intermarriages would not be authorized to sit on the board. But today the situation has changed; there are mixed married Jewish partners on the boards of most Jewish bodies (e.g. Youth Organization, Board of Delegates) except the Hevrah Kadisha (religious burial society). Children of mixed marriages attend the Jewish day school in large numbers.

All Finnish Jews recognized as Jews by the halacha or through halachic conversions, are members of the community. In the past, conversions were completed in Denmark but now many are performed by the rabbi in Helsinki. The vast majority of Jews in Finland are members of the Jewish community and pay communal taxes, but a few Jews choose to opt out, some for financial reasons (although they often remain active in Jewish organizations) or because as children of mixed marriages they have few connections with the community. According to Finnish law, children are registered in the files of the religious community of their mothers at birth unless the parents decide otherwise and register them in the civil register. If adults opt out of the Jewish community they inform the community of their decision and request that their files be sent to the secular central population register.

Finland always has trouble securing rabbis for its small isolated community. The present rabbi, who arrived in Finland in 1968 from Hungary and Israel, served for a few years as the community's shochet (ritual slaughterer) and hazzan (cantor), before his appointment as rabbi of the Helsinki community in 1974.

The community tries to hold a daily minyan (prayer quorum), although it is sometimes difficult to do so. On Shabbat about thirty men attend services and on the high holidays there are between three hundred and five hundred worshipers. The synagogue follows Orthodox ritual. Only about ten people in the community do not drive on Shabbat. Perhaps 20 percent of Helsinki's Jews keep kosher; most of those who keep kosher homes eat dairy meals out. Kosher slaughtering is permitted in Finland and there is a kosher butcher shop in Helsinki.

There is little in the way of Jewish studies for adults, except the lesson given between the Mincha and Maariv services on Shabbat afternoons. Mostly Jewish observances reflect gut wishes to continue the traditions of one's parents, without any concommitant interest in learning more about Judaism and what the observances stand for.[5]

The community of Torku has a synagogue-Jewish Community Center and a cantor-teacher. High holiday services are conducted in Tampere.

The Organizational Structure of the Community

The three Finnish Jewish Communities are united
under the Council of Jewish Communities in Finland,
which is an affiliate of the World Jewish Congress.[6]
The Council, whose function is to represent Jewish
interests in Finland, is composed of representatives
of the three local Jewish community boards. Ad hoc
meetings are held whenever needed. In June 1976, the
Council issued a statement condemning an anti-Semitic
article that had appeared in the Helsinki press.

In 1961, a Jewish Community Center was dedicated
in Helsinki. Present at the dedication ceremony was
the wife of the Finnish President, the Israeli
Minister to Finland, and Chief Rabbi of Sweden. The
Center is characteristic of the trend among smaller
European Jewish communities toward building
"roof-type" centers offering facilities for all types
of communal services; it houses a kindergarten, an old
age home with sixteen beds, auditorium, lounge,
meeting rooms, mikvah, and a nine room school. Hot
meals are provided for the school in the Center's
kosher kitchen. The Helsinki municipality donated the
land. Money for construction expenses, totalling
$36,600,000, was raised locally, partly through a
government subvention and through a long-term loan
provided by the American Jewish Joint Distribution
Committee. The Finnish Jewish community was not
eligible for funds from the Conference on Material
Claims Against Germany, one of the large contributors
to the other Scandinavian Jewish communities.[7]

The Helsinki Jewish Coeducational School was
formed in the second decade of this century. At first
conducted by Russian immigrant teachers as a heder,
the school later added secular subjects and became a
modern day school.

In 1961, the school had one hundred thirty pupils in nine classes, which constituted approximately 80 percent of the Jewish children of elementary school age in Helsinki. By 1970, the number of students had dropped to one hundred and has been steadily declining ever since because of the low Jewish birth rate.[8]

Children attend the school for nine grades, from six through fifteen years of age. Upon graduation, children continue their studies in one of the public secondary schools, where as members of a minority religious group they are exempt from morning prayers and religion classes. If there are five Jewish students in a class, they are entitled, under law, to special Jewish religion classes, the same as other minority groups. However, because of the small Jewish population in the city and the fact that Jewish students do not attend the same secondary schools, there are seldom five Jewish students in any one class.

The day school curriculum conforms to the standard Finnish educational program. In addition, a full Jewish studies curriculum is followed, including Bible, Hebrew language, customs, history, Israel, and celebration of holidays. Both Finnish and Hebrew are used as languages of instruction. Teachers in the secular studies department are not Jewish, neither is the present headmaster of the school. The Diaspora Education Department of the Jewish Agency sends Israeli teachers to maintain the Jewish Studies program. One of the difficulties is the lack of sufficient educational material in Finnish.

The school meets at the Community Center, adjacent to the synagogue. Half the school's expenses are met by the government (Ministry of Education) and the municipality; the other half is met through community financing, which calls for about half the community's budget, and through tuition fees. At present over 80 percent of the Jewish children in Helsinki still attend the school.

The Finnish educational system is now in the process of changing over to an elementary, junior and senior high program, where free education will be provided for the first nine years. The Helsinki Jewish Coeducational School has entered into an agreement with the government under which the government will heavily subsidize the school. It was feared that a problem would arise as to whether control of the school would remain in the hands of the Jewish community or not and whether non-Jews would be admitted as students, but under terms of the agreement the student body is to remain Jewish and control will be maintained by the community.

Jewish kindergartens are in operation in Helsinki and Turku. No formal Jewish studies are available for secondary school students.

The Zionist Federation is quite active, mainly in conducting public relations on Israel's behalf in both the Jewish and non-Jewish communities. It uses the Youth Organization and Academic Jewish Club to present its philosophy in debates where a direct representative of the Zionist Federation would be expected to take a Zionist stand. The Zionist Federation also helps potential olim (immigrants to Israel), acting as an intermediary for them with various agencies in Israel. Israel Independence Day celebrations, as well as occasional films and lectures, are under the patronage of the Zionist Federation. Zionist youth groups, other than a small Bnei Akiva group in Turka, do not function in Finland; instead, young Zionists sit on the Board of the Zionist Federation itself.

WIZO groups exist in Helsinki and Turku today; prior to this groups also functioned in Viborg and Tampera, and when they disbanded, individual members joined the groups in Helsinki and Turku. Helsinki WIZO was founded in 1926 with a membership of twenty-five. As of 1970, it had two hundred and one members, including eight from Tampere. Its activities include occasional Hebrew courses, lectures on Israel and Judaism, celebration of Jewish holidays and

143

participation in the annual World WIZO Bible Day. Aviv groups for younger women have recently been formed, and Jewish brides automatically receive free membership for one year. Turku WIZO was founded in 1922, with a membership of thirty five. In 1970, all eighty seven Jewish women in the community were members of WIZO, the only adult Zionist organization in the community. Its activities are similar to the ones in Helsinki. Every Jewish girl in Turku receives one year's free membership in WIZO upon reaching her twenty-first birthday. The two WIZO organizations -- in Helsinki and Turku -- jointly sponsor a WIZO Day Creche in Shaviv Israel and contribute to the "Sponsor a Child" fund. Annual WIZO campaigns are held in both cities. Helsinki WIZO is represented in the Zionist Federation of Finland and the non-Jewish Council of Finnish Women; it also always sends delegates to the biennial Scandinavian WIZO Conferences.[9]

The Youth and Pioneering Department of the Zionist Organization carries on marginal youth work in Finland, the community being too small to justify sending a permanent shaliach to work there. However, the shaliach to Sweden has responsibility for frequent visits to Finland and whenever lecturers or artists are sent to the larger Scandinavian Jewish communities, efforts are made to have them visit the smaller communities, such as Finland. It is hoped that the next Israeli teacher sent to the Helsinki Jewish Coeducational school will officially work with students and youth in the community.[10]

In principle, every Jew with an academic degree or any Jew studying for one is eligible for membership in the Academic Jewish Club, regardless of age. All young people in the community between twelve and twenty five years of age are automatically members of the Youth Organization.

The Youth Organization meets irregularly for discussion groups and lectures. Chief Rabbi Bent Melchior of Denmark delivers lecture-seminars to the group twice a year and Bnei Akiva occasionally sends shlichim to lecture. Various adult members of the

144

community also serve as speakers. Its social program, which is more extensive than its cultural program, includes frequent hikes, skiing trips, dances, and an annual party for the whole community. The group is an affiliate of the pan-Scandinavian Youth Federation (SJUF). Youth Organization meetings are held in a special clubroom at the Community Center (other groups share clubrooms). The Youth Organization Board meets weekly and activities are held approximately every twenty days. A Youth Organization group also exists in Turku, and there are sometimes inter-community activities.

The Academic Jewish Club is not very active, mainly serving as an outlet for individuals doing propaganda work for the Jewish people to the non-Jewish community, especially the academic world. An affiliate of the World Union of Jewish Students (WUJS), the club sends members to international WUJS meetings and in 1970 sponsored a WUJS winter seminar for two hundred participants in Helsinki. The Jewish Academic Club is also an affiliate of the Nordic Jewish Student Association (NOIS). Although it has very few activities directed to the Jewish student body, the group has been quite active in the struggle for Soviet Jewry.

A small Bnei Akiva group functions in Turku, where there is a tendency toward more marked religious identification.

The Community Center houses a Jewish libary. Recently a group has been formed of individuals interested in researching the history of the Jewish community in Finland. A non-Jewish history professor has been commissioned to write the book.

A B'nai Brith lodge was set up in Helsinki in 1961. It is part of the pan-Scandinavian B'nai Brith Council and its members receive B'nai Brith Nyet, the Scandinavian B'nai Brith magazine published in Denmark.

The Makkabi Sports Club meets at the Community Center, having given up its private facilities when the Center was built. Officially the club is open to both youth and adults, but the only active adult activity is the bowling league. About thirty young people are active Makkabi members. A generation ago Makkabi was an active cultural and social organization throughout Scandinavia and many of the present leaders of the Finnish Jewish community, especially those who influence the Helsinki community budget and allocations to organizations, still identify with the club and give it their support.[11]

The Hevra Kadisha (religious burial society) is the only autonomous body within the community. To be elected to its board is considered an honor in the community. A number of younger people, usually from traditional Jewish homes, have become active on the board.

Small social welfare groups have been in existence for years. The Bikur Cholim Society runs a hospital in the Community Center, combined with the Old Age Home there. Before the Center was built it had similar facilities. In the past, when there were more poor people in the community, they went to the Bikur Cholim doctor. Members of the society also visit Jews confined in Finnish hospitals.

Originally, the Gemilut Hesed Fund was established to help the indigent. Today it grants loans to individuals and small businesses. Another small loan fund is the Hachnassot Kalah Veorchim Fund, originally intended to provide dowries for poor brides and care for transients. WIZO also carries on social welfare activities in the community. Generally, women participating in the Bikur Cholim and Gemilut Hesed organizations are older than those in WIZO and are not Zionist oriented.

Community members pay an annual community tax. Almost all Jewish organizations are financed by the community, although each is registered with the government as an autonomous body. Bikur Cholim,

146

Hachnasot Kalah and Makkabi receive more community support than most groups. The Youth Organization and the Academic Jewish Club, like all youth groups in Finland, receive support from the Ministry of Education and Culture. The women's groups and sports group are also state-subsidized. the Helsinki Jewish Coeducational School receives government funds. The Magbit holds an annual campaign in Finland, in which it approaches large donors individually and organizes a cultural fund-raising evening.

Governance of the Community

Two bodies govern the Jewish community: the
Board of Representatives (Seurakunta Valtuvsto) and
the Board of Governors (Hallintononeuvsto).

The Board of Representatives is elected at an
open meeting of the community every four years. In
the history of the community there have been only two
cases of lists formed on political grounds: once when
the Youth Organization sponsored a list in 1970-71 and
once in 1966-67, when a group was formed to support a
religious platform. Even in those cases there were no
organized parties, but rather groups of individuals
who decided to run together. Usually there is a list
of individual candidates, not all of whom are even
known well by all the community members, and there is
no election campaign designed to introduce them.

Twenty eight members sit on the Board of
Representatives. The board meets two or three times a
year for general debates and to approve the budget.
It also elects representatives to some Jewish
organizations.

The Board of Governors is a seven-to-nine member
body elected by the Board of Representatives. Each
member has a special area of interest, but the body as
a whole votes on all issues and governs the day to day
affairs of the Community. The Board of Governors
proposes lists of candidates for the boards of the
school and the hospital to the Board of
Representatives for final approval. The Governors
meet weekly. Many of its members also sit on the
Board of Representatives.

Voting age in the community is eighteen and that
is also the minimum age for candidates. Elected
representatives are often from a core group of
families active in many organizations. There seems to

149

be a correlation between wealth and community status, with an exception being for younger people, who are becoming known in professional fields. The core of leadership remains the same, with other leaders constantly added on to it or deleted from it. About ten years ago a shift took place in the leadership ranks, power being transferred from the oldest leadership group (over sixty years of age) to the fifty-to-sixty age bracket. Recently another change has begun, quickly lowering the leadership age to include many more leaders in the twenty five to thirty five age group. Community members thirty five to forty five years old are conspicuous not only in their absence from leadership but also from community activities in general.

Relations With Other Communities

Close social ties exist among community leaders in all the Nordic communities and date back to their days of activity in the Scandinavian Youth Federation and Maccabi. Pan-Scandinavian bodies include the Scandinavian Youth Federation, the Pan-Scandinavian Zionist Organization, the Scandinavian B'nai Brith Council, Scandinavian Bnei Akiva, Pan-Nordic WIZO Council, and Nordic Jewish Students Association (NOIS).

Finland was the third nation, after the United States and the Union of Soviet Socialist Republics, to recognize the State of Israel in 1948. Twenty-nine of its Jewish youth fought in the War of Independence and over one hundred Finnish Jews have emigrated to Israel. There is very strong support for Israel in the Jewish community, especially among its older people. Younger leaders appear to have a more critical attitude toward Israel and have been in conflict with the other over whether to allocate more funds for Israel or direct them back into the local community.

GLOSSARY OF HEBREW TERMS

aliyah--literally means ascent or the act of going up; refers to the immigration of Jews to Israel.

bar mitzvah--a synagogue ceremony marking the 13th birthday of a Jewish boy acquiring religious responsibility.

bet din--a religious court comprised of three rabbis

halachic--pertaining to Jewish oral and written law

haskalah--an intellectual enlightenment movement among Jews of eastern Europe in the 18th and 19th centuries

hazzan--a cantor

heder--elementary school for Jewish religious instruction

kabbalistic--pertaining to mystical interpretation of the Scriptures which was originally developed orally among Jewish rabbis beginning in the 12th century

minyan--a quorum of at least ten males above the age of thirteen necessary for Jewish worship

mohel (pl. mohalim)--a ritual circumciser

shaliach (pl. shlichim)--emissary

shochet (pl. shochatim)--an officially licensed slaughterer of animals and poultry according to Jewish law

The Jewish Community of Sweden

1. "Scandinavia's Jewish Communities," American Scandinavian Review, p. 128; Pamphlet of the Jewish Community of Stockholm, 1964; Encyclopedia Judaica, Vol. XV, pp. 545-547; Naomi Ben-Asher, "Jewish Life in Scandinavia: Sweden," in Congress Weekly, Dec. 23, 1957, p. 9.

2. Encyclopedia Judaica, op. cit., p. 547.

3. David Schwarz, "A Study of the Attitudes Held by Members of the Swedish Parliament on Ethnic Minorities and Immigration to Sweden, Report No. 1," Pedagogic Institute, University of Stockholm, 1968, Summary, 1169, p. 37; Encyclopedia Judaica, op. cit., p. 548; Review Draft of the Study of European Jewish Communities, Abraham Kessler, ed., 1964, p.1.

4. Jewish Chronicle, March 10, 1950. p.1.

5. Schwarz, op. cit., p. 37.

6. Ibid. The Jewish Community was bound to pay for indigent Jews arriving. The Community complained that the Russian Jews "were not on the level of education that can be compatible with the true interests of the country to allow them a fixed place of residence here."

7. Ibid.

8. Encyclopedia Judaica, loc. cit.; Kessler, loc. cit.

9. Allen Pollack, "Jews in Sweden," in Dispersion and Unity, 1961, pp. 54-55; Fred Werbell,

"Jews in Sweden," in Jewish Communal Services, 1964, pp. 113-114; Maurice Perlzweig, "Salute to Sweden," in Jewish Frontier, May 5, 1946, pp. 31-33.

10. Encyclopedia Judaica, loc. cit., p. 550.

11. Jewish Chronicle, May 16, 1947, p. 9; July 15, 1947, p. 11; Aug. 15, 1947, p. 9.

12. Pollack, loc. cit., p. 54; Encyclopedia Judaica, loc. cit.

13. Encyclopedia Judaica, loc. cit.; Pollack, loc. cit.

14. Ibid.

15. The following is a list of immigration figures from Sweden compiled by the Israel Central Bureau of Statistics, as of 1974: until 1951 - 96; 1951 - 13; 1953 - 12; 1954 - 0; 1955 - 11; 1956 - 2; 1957 - 2; 1958 - 12; 1959 - 5; 1960 - 13; 1961 - 8; 1962 - 10; 1963 - 21; 1964 -26; 1965 - 13; 1966 -14; 1967 - 6; 1968 - 8; 1969 - 12 immigrants and 24 temporary residents; 1970 - 14 immigrants and 55 temporary residents; 1971 - 17 immigrants and 48 temporary residents.

16. Proceedings of the 7th International Convention of the World Council of Synagogues, 1968, address by Rabbi Morton Narrowe, p. 21.

17. Interview of Mr. Yitzhak Shomron, Jewish Agency shaliach to Sweden, 1970-1973; April, 1974.

18. Pollack, loc. cit., pp. 55-56.

19. Proceedings of the 9th International Convention of the World Council of Synagogues, 1972, address by Rabbi Morton Narrowe, pp. 31-32.

20. Interview with Rabbi Moshe Edelman, Communities Division, Scandinavian Desk, Jewish Agency, November, 1975; Ben-Asher, op. cit., p. 11.

21. Interview of Mr. Max Varom, ex-Israel Ambassador to Sweden, May, 1974.

22. Schwarz, op. cit., p. 35.

23. Egenie Soderberg, "Sweden Against Anti-Semitism," in Jewish Frontier, Dec., 1943, pp. 29-30; Jewish Chronicle, Jan. 14, 1949, p. 11.

24. Pollack, op. cit., p. 68; Jewish Chronicle, Aug. 28, 1952, p. 1; Sept. 12, 1952, p. 14.

25. Jewish Chronicle, Jan. 14, 1955, p. 28; Bulletin on Antisemitic Events, no. 25, April, 1974, p. 55.

26. Pollack, op. cit., pp. 68-69.

27. Schwarz, op. cit., pp. 21-22, 35-36

28. Bulletin on Antisemitic Events, no. 26, April 1975, p. 70; Jewish Chronicle, Oct. 28, 1960, p. 40.

29. Varom Interview.

30. Schwarz, op. cit., p. 37. "To quote the Minister of Welfare of the Swedish Government, Mr. Moller, when, in an address to the Swedish Parliament in January, 1945, he tried to defend the very restrictive Jewish immigration policy, saying: 'The Swedish Government with regard to letting Jews come into the country was at least as generous as the Jewish community in Stockholm'."

31. Ibid., p. 38.

32. Liva Herz, "Notes on Identificational Assimilation Among Forty Jews in Malmo," in the Jewish Journal of Sociology, XI, pp. 2, 19, 165-174.

33. Edelman Interview.

34. Varom Interview.

35. Edelman Interview.

36. Interview of Mr. Moshe Apellblat, Kristianstad and Stockholm communities, NOIS, SJUF, Swedish Zionist Federation.

37. Mosaiska Forsamlingen i Stockholm, Annual Report, 1973, p. 20.

38. Edelman Interview.

39. Pollack, op. cit., p. 56.

40. Interview of Ms. Yocheved Zusman, Information Department, Jewish Agency, December, 1975; Apellblat Interview.

41. Zusman Interview.

42. Edelman Interview; Jewish Chronicle, May 27, 1949, p. 10; Aug. 24, 1956, p. 10.

43. Apellblat Interview.

44. Mosaiska,loc. cit., p. 1. Although there was an increase in membership in 1973, because of the high death rate, the number of members decreased from 5,006 in 1972 to 4,970 in 1973.

45. Interview of Dr. Bruno Kaplan, January, 1969.

46. Varom Interview.

47. Mosaiska, loc. cit.

48. Letters from Yitzhak Shomron to Mordechai Bar - On, 18.4.72; 30.3.73; Mosaiska, loc. cit., pp. 39-40.

49. Mosaiska, loc. cit.

50. Jewish Chronicle, Dec. 7, 1962, p. 21.

51. Interview of Mr. Norman Zysblat, director, British Desk, Youth and Pioneering Department, Jewish Agency, December, 1975.

52. Apellblat Interview.

53. Apellblat Interview.

54. Mosaiska, loc. cit.

55. Pollack, op. cit., p. 57.

56. Interview of Mr. Mordecai Speir, Stockholm Jewish Community, November, 1975.

57. Interview of Rabbi Aryeh Linker, Stockholm Orthodox Congregations, November, 1975.

58. Edelman Interview.

59. Speir Interview.

60. Mosaiska, loc. cit., p. 34.

61. Ibid., p. 30.

62. Forsamlingsbladet, Jewish Community of Stockholm, 1964.

63. Werbell, op. cit., p. 114.

64. Mosaiska, loc. cit.

65. Edelman Interview.

66. Mosaiska, loc. cit.

67. Kessler, op. cit., p. 4.

68. Mosaiska, op. cit., pp. 36-37.

69. Ibid; Pollack, loc. cit., pp. 60-61.

70. Study of Jewish Education in the Diaspora, ed. Alexander Dushkin, WZO, 1971, p. 7.

71. Schwarz, op. cit., pp. 36-37, footnote no. 3.

72. Pollack, op. cit., pp. 62-63.

73. Edelman Interview.

74. Pollack, op. cit., p. 61; Mosaiska, loc. cit., pp. 43-44.

75. Ibid.

76. Apellblat Interview, World Council, 7th Convention, pp. 23-24.

77. Mosaiska, op. cit.

78. Edelman Interview.

79. Interview of Rabbi Morton Narrowe, June, 1970; World Council, 9th Convention, loc. cit.

80. Varom Interview.

81. Zysblat Interview.

82. Zysblat Interview.

83. Edelman, Zysblat, Apellblat, Speir Interviews.

84. Zysblat, Edelman, Apellblat and Zusman Interviews.

85. Mosaiska, op. cit., p. 56, p. 59; Letter from Shomron to Bar - On, 18·4·72.

86. Pollack, op. cit., pp. 67-68; Zysblat, Apellblat, Edelman, Speir Interviews.

87. Zysblat, Apellblat Interviews.

88. Varom Interview.

89. Shomron Interview.

90. Mosaiska, op. cit., pp. 39-40.

91. Saga of a Movement; WIZO, 1920-1970, pp. 104-106.

92. Varom Interview.

93. Mosaiska, op. cit., p. 60; Apellblat Interview.

94. Bernard K. Johnpoll, "Polish Jews in Scandinavia," in Midstream, February, 1974, p. 55.

95. Kessler, op. cit., pp. 6-12.

96. Ibid., p. 15.

97. J.N.F. News, Autumn, 1975.

98. Pollack, op. cit., p. 56; Edelman, Apellblat Interviews.

99. World Council, 9th Convention, op. cit., p. 32.

100. Zysblat Interview.

101. Varom, Shomron Interviews.

102. Edelman Interview.

103. Ernest Stock, "Jewish Multicountry Associations," in American Jewish Year Book, Volume 75, 1974-1975, pp. 591-592.

104. Zysblat Interview.

THE JEWISH COMMUNITY OF DENMARK

1. Harold Flender, Rescue of Danish Jewry (W.H. Allen, London, 1963), p. 4; Dov Levitan, unpublished seminar paper, Bar-Ilan University, 1976, p. 1, footnote 2 (Michael Hartwig, Jodeine in Denmark, Copenhagen, 1952).

2. Ibid., p. 5.

3. Max Awner, "Diaspora in Denmark," in Jewish Frontier, Vol. XXV, no. 6, June 1958, pp. 9-10.

4. Ibid., p. 16.

5. Flender, op. cit., p. 14.

6. Ibid., p. 6.

7. Ibid., p. 10.

8. Ibid., pp. 18-20.

9. Ibid., p. 21.

10. Ibid., p. 26.

11. Encyclopedia Judaica, Vol. 5, (Keter Pub., Jerusalem, 1971), p. 1541.

12. Flender, op. cit., pp. 11-12.

13. Awner, loc. cit., p. 9.

14. Interview with Rabbi Michael Melchior, Jerusalem, April 1976.

15. Flender, op. cit., p. 4.

16. Ibid., p. 9.

17. Ibid., p. 11.

18. According to Jacques Blum's study of Danish Jewish affiliation <u>Danske</u> <u>og/eller</u> <u>Jøde</u>; published in Copenhagen in 1972 and quoted in Levittan's paper (p. 9), the figure is approximately 33% with the majority of such marriage partners Jewish men and Christian women.

19. Levittan, <u>op</u>. <u>cit</u>., p. 9.

20. Interview of Mrs. Marianne Amir, Jerusalem, January 1976.

21. Flender, <u>op</u>. <u>cit</u>., p. 5.

22. <u>Ibid</u>., p. 7.

23. <u>Ibid</u>., p. 17.

24. <u>Ibid</u>., p. 19.

25. <u>Jewish</u> <u>Chronicle</u>, January 20, 1961, p. 19.

26. <u>Jewish</u> <u>Chronicle</u>, February 8, 1952, p. 11; September 4, 1953, p. 32; April 15, 1950, p. 13; January 20, 1961, p. 12.

27. Victor Bienstock, "There's a Jewish Dilemma in Denmark: Polish Emigres," in the <u>National</u> <u>Jewish</u> <u>Monthly</u>, November 1970, p. 47.

28. <u>Ibid</u>., p. 48.

29. Interview of Mr. Norman Zysblat, Jerusalem, February, 1976.

30. Martin Schiff, "Polish Jewish Refugees in Scandinavia," in <u>Midstream</u>, Vol. XVIII, no. 2, February 1971, p. 40.

31. Zysblat interview.

32. Interview of Rabbi Bent Melchior, Jerusalem, January 1976.

33. Flender, op. cit., pp. 7-8.

34. Interview of Mrs. Marcus (Metta) Melchior, Rabbi Michael Melchior, April 1976.

35. Jewish Chronicle, July 2, 1954, p. 15; November 19, 1954, p. 14.

36. Melchior interview.

37. Melchior interview.

38. Rafael Edelmann, "Royal Library of Copenhagen," in Jewish Book Annual, pp. 39-43.

39. The Saga of a Movement, WIZO, 1920-1970, Wizo, 1971.

40. Levittan, op. cit., p. 14.

41. Flender, op. cit., p. 14.

42. Levittan, op. cit., p. 17.

Jewish Community of Norway

1. Oscar Mendelshon, Jodenes Historie i Norege Gjennom 300 Ar (Oslo: Universitetsforlaget, 1969).

2. On the bureaucracy see: J. Higley, K. Brofoss, K.G. Roholt, "The Civil Service of Norway," Monograph published by the Department of Political Science, Oslo University.

3. Mendelshon, op. cit., pp. 29-31.

4. English translation from Samuel Abrahamsen, "The Exclusion Clause of Jews in the Norwegian Constitution of May 17, 1814," in Jewish Social Studies, Vol. 30 (April 1968), p. 68.

5. Ibid., p. 44.

6. Information on political behavior influenced by religious values can be found in the following works: Henry Valen, "Regional Contracts in Norwegian Politics: A Review of Data from Official Statistics and from Sample Surveys" in E. Allardt and Y. Littunen (eds.), Cleavages, Ideologies and Party Systems, (Helsinki, 1964); Henry Valen and Daniel Katz, Political Parties in Norway, (Oslo, Universitetsforlaget, 1967); Thor Hall, "Religious Arguments and Attitudes in Denmark and Norway Relative to the Referenda Concerning Membership in the EEC," Monograph published by the Department of Philosophy and Religion, University of Tennessee at Chattanooga, undated. This interesting study deals with the influence of religious values and perception on political behavior in the farming districts of Norway, as reflected in a referendum conducted in 1972. In this referendum, the Norwegian public voted against the entry of Norway into the Common Market.

The results of the referendum were: 53.5%
against entry into the Common Market and 46.5%
in favor. The study demonstrates that 62% of
the population living in the farming districts
and influenced by Protestant values voted
against.

7. Samuel Abrahamsen, "The Exclusion Clause of
    Jews in the Norwegian Constitution of May 17,
    1814," Jewish Social Studies, Vol. 30, April
    1968, p. 18. This study is devoted to the
    struggle of the poet Wergeland for the rights
    of the Jews and contains many selections from
    his poems translated into English.

8. Mendelshon, op. cit., pp. 61-114.

9. Falsen's response was originally published in
    the Norwegian newspaper Den Norske Tilskuer,
    Bergen, nos. 41 and 42, October 6, 1817, pp.
    334-336. English translation from Abrahamsen,
    op. cit., p. 81.

10. Abrahamsen, op. cit., p. 72.

11. Ibid., p. 70.

12. Mendelshon, op. cit., pp. 131-132.

13. Abrahamsen, op. cit., p. 79.

14. Mendelshon, op. cit., pp. 264-265.

15. Abrahamsen, op. cit., p. 77.

16. On the beginning of Jewish immigration to
    Norway see Mendelshon, op. cit., pp. 277-306.

17. These figures appear in Mendelshon's study and
    are integrated here into a table.

18. Otto Hauglin, "Religionen" in Natalie Rogoff
    Ramsy (ed.), Det Norske Samfunn (Oslo:
    Gyldendal Norsk Forlag, 1975), pp. 584-613.

19. Mendelshon, op. cit., p. 280.

20. Daniel J. Elazar, "The Kehillah," Monograph published by the Department of Political Studies, Bar-Ilan University (Ramat-Gan, 1976).

21. David Rodnick, The Norwegians: A Study in National Culture (Washington, D.C.: Public Affairs Press, 1951), p. 18.

22. There is a slight tendency for contemporary Norwegians to leave the state church--at a rate of only 0.1 percent per year.

23. Hauglin, op. cit., p. 601.

24. Mendelshon, op. cit., p. 451.

25. On the disputes centered around the cemetery, see Mendelshon, op. cit., pp. 449-452.

26. Ibid., p. 438.

27. Ibid., p. 545.

28. For a comprehensive account of the prohibition of ritual slaughter in Norway, see Mendelshon, op. cit., pp. 570-583.

29. "Norway" in The Universal Jewish Encyclopedia, p. 242.

30. Ibid.

31. Mendelshon op. cit., p. 628.

32. Ibid.

33. Ibid., p. 603.

34. The Jewish Chronicle, April 27, 1951.

35. Ibid., September 19, 1952.

36. Encyclopedia Judaica, p. 1226.

37. Statistical Yearbook of Norway (Oslo: Central Bureau of Statistics, 1974), p. 13.

38. Ibid.

39. Johan Galtung, "Norway in the World Community," in Natalie Rogoff Ramsy (ed.), The Norwegian Society, (Oslo University Press, 1974), p. 394.

40. Yearly report of the Board of Representatives for 1975. Det Mosaiske Trossamfund. Oslo. Rundskriv no. 4, May 12, 1976.

41. Galtung, op. cit., pp. 401-402.

42. Hauglin, op. cit., p. 613.

Finland

1. Encyclopedia Judaica, Vol. 6, Jerusalem: Keter
   Publishing Co., 1971, pp. 1295-1298; S. Ralph
   Cohen, "Scandinavia's Jewish Communities," in
   American-Scandinavian Review, (date unknown),
   p. 130; Yehude Levine, "Long Twilight: The Jews
   of Finland," in Congress Bi-Weekly, Vol. 32,
   No. 5, March 1, 1965, pp. 10-12.

2. Encyclopedia Judaica, Ibid., p. 1298; American
   Jewish Year Book, Vol. 63, 1962-63, p. 327;
   Vol. 75, pp. 562-563; Interview of Mr. Joel
   Blankette, June, 1976.

3. Blankette Interview.

4. Blankette Interview.

5. Blankette Interview.

6. Jewish Communities of the World, Third Revised
   Edition, 1971, Institute for Jewish
   Affairs/WJC, Andre Deutch, ed., pp. 89-90.

7. AJYB, op. cit., p. 333.

8. Deutch, op. cit.,; Blankette Interview.

9. Saga of a Movement, WIZO 1920-1970, WIZO, 1971.

10. Interview of Mr. Norman Zysblat, Director,
    British Desk, Youth and Pioneering Department,
    February, 1976.

11. Blankette Interview.

ABOUT THE AUTHORS

Daniel J. Elazar is overall director of the Study of Jewish Community Organization. Among his various responsibilities, he is President of the Jerusalem Center for Public Affairs, Senator N.M. Patterson Professor of Intergovernmental Relations at Bar-Ilan University, and Senior Fellow of the Center for the Study of Federalism at Temple University. He is the author or editor of numerous books and articles in the field of Jewish political studies, including the recently published <u>Gazetteer of Jewish Political Organization</u> and <u>Kinship and Consent: The Jewish Political Tradition and its Contemporary Manifestations</u>.

Adina Weiss Liberles was one of the original research associates of the Center for Jewish Community Studies, where she was permanently attached to the Study of Jewish Community Organization. She has an M.A. in contemporary Jewish studies from Brandeis University. Among her other contributions to the worldwide study is a major report on the Jewish community of Belgium and studies of the Danish, Finnish, and Swedish Jewish communities.

Simcha Werner is a political scientist presently teaching at the University of Manitoba. He was a former lecturer in public administration at Bar-Ilan University and has published widely in that field. Dr. Werner earned his M.A. at the University of Oslo and his Ph.D. at Temple University. He undertook this study while a research assistant of the Center for Jewish Community Studies.

173